POORER RICHARD'S AMERICA

WHAT WOULD BEN SAY?

POORER RICHARD'S AMERICA
WHAT WOULD BEN SAY?

TOM BLAIR

*It is the easiest thing in the world
for a Man to deceive himself.*
—Poor Richard's Almanack, *April 1746*

So it be for a Nation.
—Poorer Richard's America, *September 2010*

SKYHORSE PUBLISHING

Skyhorse Publishing books may be purchased in bulk at special discounts for sales promotion, corporate gifts, fund-raising, or educational purposes. Special editions can also be created to specifications. For details, contact the Special Sales Department, Skyhorse Publishing, 555 Eighth Avenue, New York, NY 10018 or info@skyhorsepublishing.com.

www.skyhorsepublishing.com

10 9 8 7 6 5 4 3 2

Library of Congress Cataloging-in-Publication Data is available on file.
ISBN: 978-1-61608-190-4

Printed in the United States of America

CONTENTS

FOREWORD

BY TOM BROKAW

Who among us has not wondered what the Founding Fathers of this unique democratic republic and free-market economy would think of what their dream has become?

George Washington, the stern father of the country, who had the air of majesty but rejected the temptations of royalty. Mr. Jefferson, the poet of liberty and champion of governing from the bottom up and not the top down. Hamilton, the boy wonder financial genius who, through the force of his intellect and oratory, gave the fledgling nation a central nervous system for its economy. John Adams, the passionate advocate with the great legal mind and even greater patriot's heart.

And, of course, Benjamin Franklin, journalist, printer, politician, sage, scientist, diplomat, raconteur, iconoclast, ladies' man, and, most of all, the quintessential American then and even now.

Walter Isaacson, in his award-winning biography, *Benjamin Franklin: An American Life*, describes him as the founding father who winks at us. His combination of wit and wisdom is best distilled, of course, in his *Poor Richard's Almanack*, which he began publishing in 1732 as a means of making money and promoting virtue.

It was an instant success, outselling even the Bible, and it lives on today as a model of topical and enduring humor, practical information such as the tidal charts, weather, eclipses, and lunar phases.

However, the genius of Franklin was his ability to see complex issues with great clarity and convey to mass audiences a simple road map to understanding. His many observations grew out of his own youthful effort to design a set of virtues by which he would lead his own life.

Among them:

Temperance: "Eat not to dullness; drink not to elevation."

Frugality: "Make no expense but to do good to others or yourself."

Industry: "Lose no time; always be employed in something useful; cut off all unnecessary actions."

There were thirteen virtues in all and they in turn led to a lifelong trail of Benjamin Franklin aphorisms that are so familiar and remain so relevant that they can help us navigate personal goals and national interests more than two centuries later.

As the *New York Times* columnist David Brooks has observed, "They are not particularly spiritual virtues but they are practical and they are democratic."

Who has not been told, "Early to bed, early to rise makes a man healthy, wealthy, and wise?" Franklin was not above refining the work of others or old folk sayings and making them sharper, and, in so doing, more useful.

"Little strokes fell great oaks."

"The cat in gloves catches no mice."

"He's a fool who makes his doctor his heir."

"Love your enemies for they will tell you your faults."

In this ambitious book by Tom Blair, *Poorer Richard's America*, we're invited to ponder what Benjamin Franklin might think of our common virtues and national direction now, in the beginning of the twenty-first century, when many of the hubristic assumptions of twentieth-century America are under siege.

Mr. Blair skillfully weaves his own thoughts on financial excesses, national will, journalism, entertainment, generational legacies, and the popular culture with the real and imagined reflections of his hero, Benjamin Franklin.

It is a provocative undertaking and, in the spirit of Franklin's mischievous manner, it is designed to at once make us think about the many ways in which we lost our way and how a daily inventory of time-tested virtues can help show us the way once again to a firm foundation built on higher ground.

"No gains without pains."

"When the well's dry we know the worth of water."

"There was never a good knife made of bad steel."

Franklin was not always a popular figure. His tart tongue, agnosticism, and flair for self-serving publicity earned him a full quota of critics and even enemies. When he died, John Adams, who long had been a critic and yet a friend of Franklin, wrote that he "had a great genius, original, sagacious, and inventive . . . He had talents for irony, allegory, and fable that he could adapt with great skill to the promotion of moral and political truth."

Tom Blair rightly asks, "Where is our Benjamin Franklin, and why aren't we listening to the original?"

—TOM BROKAW
JULY 2010

INTRODUCTION

KIND READER,

For two centuries, plus two decades, I have been observing you with utmost fascination and, at times, unfettered amazement . . . a stroll on the moon, who would have dreamt. While I am foremost proud of you, and think proudly of myself as one of you, of late I have become heavy with worry. For many Americans, the fire in the belly no longer seems to burn. More and more of you cling tight to the Great Federal Breast while beseeching your government to kiss your hurts and chase the pain away. But alas, the pain is increasing as your government casts future generations adrift in a sea of debt. Dear citizens, both your finances and your nation's are capsized and sinking by the stern. Your credit cards . . . I thought lightning was frightful . . . mortgages and the National Debt are screaming in agony. Meanwhile, insecure elected officials spew forth vile declarations crafted to demonize their opposition in hopes of positioning themselves for reelection . . . thus ensuring for themselves a player's role and costume on the Nation's Stage of Tragedy.

> *Here comes the orator, with his flood of words, and his drop of reason.*
> —Poor Richard's, *October 1735*

Not wishing to pummel, but rather to propel you, let me acknowledge what a truly admirable nation of citizens populate America. You are generous. Generous with your money and your time. Always ready to help another country's citizens. When attacked, you strive to win; then, once victorious, you rebuild your defeated opponent. The contentment of another nation is not your discontentment. For most Americans, a healthy and loving family is still the greatest treasure. And, as always, Americans are prepared to toil diligently for a fair day's pay.

Now for the grim news. My dear America may well have touched its majestic zenith, thus being poised to begin its slide from grace. With a quick shrug, many of you dismiss my pleading; why not, when in booming voices politicians boast, "America is the greatest nation the world has ever seen"? Certainly to the ear their trumpeting is quite reassuring—as reassuring as were the British statesmen of my generation smugly claiming that "Britannia rules the waves . . ." Alas, two hundred years later, Britannia, with its cracked spars, tattered sails, and rotting hull, sits idle, moored to the dock of past greatness.

The golden age is never the present age.
—Poor Richard's, *December 1750*

A glance back, if we may. During the first two centuries of America's existence most parents struggled mightily to provide their children a better life than theirs had been. Generation after generation of parents toiled long days for the betterment of their offspring, and thus created a most wondrous by-product: a nation of agricultural abundance and industrial might. Your forefathers and foremothers didn't require a State or Federal Stimulus Package to nurture national growth; by working and sacrificing for Junior and little Missy, they forged the most robust economic engine the world has ever seen.

And there was another raw reality that shaped the early American profile. Most families ate only what they killed or grew. For my countrymen an empty belly was an uncompromising motivator for clearing fields and planting crops, pausing only to track deer or build a fish dam. Hunger was not an abstract notion for most citizens of early America; it was a lifelong partner. The absolute need to toil for next week's bread, next season's crop, next year's slaughtering, created not so much an American work ethic as a survival ethic.

So, then, permit me to ask an indelicate question: If for the past decades modern Americans haven't been tracking deer to feed the family, or saving 25 percent of hard-earned wages to make their children's future brighter than was theirs, what have they been doing? Please, by your leave, a drumroll and bow to the King. I hesitantly have concluded that conspicuous consumption has become not only a perverse addiction, but a god to many Americans, the twin cornerstones to American Consumerism being materialism and instant gratification.

Spare and have is better than spend and crave.
　　　　　　　—Poor Richard's, *August 1758*

A spattering of materialism can serve well as the grease to the wagon—sorry, truck wheels of progress—materialism being the desire for something not necessary for the enjoyment of everyday life, but providing an inner satisfaction of ego or pride. As a carrot on the end of a long stick dangling before a mule, the pursuit of a material object can motivate an individual to wondrous levels of creativity and productivity. Thus, it is the path taken to obtain a material object that causes Satan to either frown or smile. Is the coveted object attained by studious application of hard work and focused thought, or does one liquidate a retirement fund to create a transient perception of wealth . . . or worse, dear reader, borrow against future hard work with a sliver of plastic?

While your propensity to gleefully consume by shoveling on personal debt is most frightening, there is another attribute of today's generation of Americans that vexes me. It is your attitude, an attitude that encourages many to boast to the world that Americans, as a class, are the best.

As pride increases, fortunes decline.
—Poor Richard's, *August 1744*

Millions of those first citizens of America, with the cruel exception of those chained in the dark squalor of slave ships, endured hard journeys from England, Ireland, Germany, Italy, China, and other far-off lands to find the better life; or, more accurately stated, to work for the better life. America was the land of opportunity, that opportunity being that if citizens toiled until their bones ached they might be able to pull more from the land than they could have, or were allowed to, in their motherland.

It is quite true, then, dear citizens, that most of you were born American. Not to be cruel, but you merely won the world lottery of citizenship. Perchance someone buys the winning lottery ticket, he is not therefore an exceptional individual; rather, just a lucky one. Many of today's American citizens may not be exceptional, just lucky. As you would say, "Right place, right time."

Do some of you kind citizens still have fire? Yes, but not the burning-hot fire of those travelers on the *Mayflower*, or of those pioneers walking in the dust next to their covered wagons so as not to tire the oxen. Today's America shelters its citizens from those rigors and cruelties its early generations suffered. No longer does one fear starvation, typhoid fever, a whipping by the master, or twelve-hour-a-day, six-day-a-week, mind-numbing, backbreaking work in a textile mill or a blazing-hot foundry. Sharp-fanged fears of yesteryear have been displaced by a basket of less-dire concerns, many being self-inflicted materialistic worries . . . "Payments on my camper are killing me."

> He who multiplies his possessions multiplies his cares.
>
> —Poor Richard's, *September 1744*

There is yet another matter; another apprehension, another most grave worry of mine. It is the United States Congress. A Congress that too often delivers legislation crafted by an eye for what is best for the next election, not what is best for the next generation of Americans. And often what is best for the next election is the financial support of robust corporations and their relentless lobbyists.

Corporations have become the shadow fourth branch of your government. And by being such, they distort and corrupt the balance of interests and representations so carefully, so hopefully, conceived and memorialized in America's Constitution by our Nation's Founding Fathers. Recall, dear reader, that we were a nation of plowmen, hunters, craftsmen, and fishermen in 1776; no Founding Father could have envisioned that in two hundred years' time the voice of a single omnipotent corporation could mask, and thus overrule, the voices of thousands of America's citizens. If only we had written "All men and corporations are created equal."

So, fellow citizens, this is the problem . . . no, these are the problems. Many of you no longer possess a burning-hot fire in your belly. It is not necessary. You are not hungry, and you enjoy a standard of living that most other residents of the planet covet. Many of you bask in the pride of being American without making sacrifices to maintain your Country as the greatest. Your national leaders fail to sound the alarm; rather, they stand at a podium perched on a mountain of National Debt, repeating to you what they believe you want to hear while spending whatever is necessary for your support. And in the halls of Congress, often deep and reverberating corporate voices drown out the whimpered pleas of individual Americans. Meanwhile, there are a few billion folks, yes billions, in foreign lands who have fire in their bellies and are willing to struggle for a better life for themselves and their children . . . and many don't own houses or cars. Because their standard of living is dramatically below yours, they can crawl up the economic curve and become much happier while still underselling America in the international bazaar.

Only a mighty effort by its citizens will stay America's slow drift from "Greatest." Otherwise, America may slip to number two and then, perhaps, slide further down from there. Erosion of economic influence and national pride won't force the closing of shopping malls or baseball stadiums; a decline will, however, require today's Americans to do what they do not do best: be somewhat humble.

While always generous to other nations, America has at times exercised a certain arrogance on the world stage. As your economic fortunes decline, no flood of sympathy will wash ashore from other lands. Foreigners will little remember, or care, that part of your large National Debt, which America wears as lead boots in the economic footrace with other nations, was incurred by America defending the

Free World during the Cold War. Few will tally the billions and billions of foreign aid exported during the past decades. Rather, while sipping a fine Merlot, smug foreigners will condescendingly whisper, "America became lazy," "They were arrogant," "Their leaders had no fiscal discipline."

> *A rich man has many friends, some true; a poor man has few friends, all true.*
> —Poorer Richard's America, *September 2010*

So, kind sirs and ladies, while abhorrently presumptuous of me, I have taken it upon myself to sound the alarm. I do this because your contemporary elected officials have little spine for the truth, and because I am a "Real American," whatever this title may encompass, as uttered by a group of your self-anointed flag bearers who proudly boast they know those of you who are not "Real Americans."

> *Clean your finger before you point at spots.*
> —Poor Richard's, *June 1750*

So with your leave I will, by the laying of words on paper, attempt to shake you. Shake firmly to awaken you as to America's wayward course, shake you to consider what is not right, and shake you to ponder what might be, what could be . . . hoping that you will assume across your broad shoulders the mantle of responsibility for conveying to the next generations of Americans a Country no less great than the America that was bestowed upon you.

My chosen missive to convey my concerns and hopeful challenges is that with which I am most comfortable, *Poor Richard's Almanack*. For a span of twenty-five years this almanack was both written by me, under the pseudonym of Richard Saunders, and printed by me. Those initial almanacks served up by Poor Richard, the first ink pressed to paper in 1732, were written by this humble author not, as I said then, for the "publick good." Rather, *Poor Richard's Almanack* was born to this world to render my purse heavy and my mind at ease. This was done to great happiness as year after year, my Countrymen purchased, with dear pennies lifted from their purses, my almanack. Within its soft paper cover were hard facts: a true calendar of tides rising and falling, moons shining full to black, the arriving and departing of the sun, and all things necessary for the farmer, hunter, fisherman, sailor, and shopkeeper to arm himself for battle with nature and those forces that threatened a tranquil life.

On the loaf of bland facts baked into the bread of *Poor Richard's Almanack* I sprinkled cinnamon. A cinnamon of witticisms cleverly crafted to gently convey fundamental truths of life's commerce and life's passions. To many a reader these witticisms seemed to have no more stature than a court jester before a King. But as you would say, "A sugarcoated pill is easier to swallow."

Residing within each witticism was a kernel of fundamental truth. A truth so obvious that it was, for many, of no weight; hence, no need to pay it a mind or a courtesy. But these diminutive-appearing truths not acknowledged and acted upon might well, in time, rise up and smite those who did not make them honored lifelong guests. Alas, dear Americans, this be true for many of you . . . you live season to season, year to year, without the guests of reason.

As slowly I became not a young man I grew in wisdom; I was not an educated lad, so any change in wisdom could only be to my betterment. With my self-proclaimed new wisdom I undertook to burden *Poor Richard's Almanack* not only with facts and witticisms, but with topical essays penned by me—essays that spoke to the forces and prejudices of commerce, governments, religions, and peoples. New topical essays addressing these same issues are, I trust, the thick bones of this narrative.

What follows is *Poorer Richard's America*, written for today's citizens of America. Please, let me beg your pardon. Truly I know how immodest it is of me to pen essays that expound upon your faults and problems. I take this presumption to my bosom and suffer the honest criticism that is due because I love America so . . . I was there for its birth. And truly, I love all Americans. No more noble people have walked God's good Earth. But your greatness, your generosity, your quick rush to right all wrongs, and your intolerance of the suffering of others will in time extinguish your ability to exercise America's most exquisite nobility.

Know well, dear reader, that those kindhearted, benevolent qualities of America, those sterling attributes that are such a part of your greatness, will, if not bridled with financial restraint and reasonableness, cause "Greatest" to slowly fade from our Country's honored title.

If emotion drives, let reason hold the reins.
—Poor Richard's, *May 1749*

Thy obliged friend and fellow citizen.

NOTES TO THE READER

While I have observed our America with keen and curious interest these past centuries, and while most happenings and occurrences I understood and easily took to my head, there were those that perplexed my logic, and no matter how diligently I applied myself I could not make sense of. Such topics of confounding facts and occasions include baseball's designated hitter rule, Paris Hilton, and credit-default-swap spreads; just a few of multitudes. So with your leave anticipated, I did petition one of yours to clarify and amplify those things most mystifying to me. And to assure that this missive is contemporary in terminology and speech, this kind gentleman translated and otherwise fashioned my many words to your ear, lest you laugh a confused laugh when you lay your eyes upon my writings.

His mirth not from pleasure, 'tis from pity of me.
                                        —*Author unknown*

The essays of this narrative are punctuated by short, pithy sayings; if you wish to startle your acquaintances with brilliance, refer to them as apothegms. Most of the sayings quoted herewith first appeared in the *Poor Richard's Almanacks* of the 1700s; and, while certainly much has changed in our America since the last *Poor Richard's Almanack* was printed in 1758, these apothegms of long ago show that man's hopes, fears, and follies have not.

During my life it was my most serious desire to express myself with modest diffidence, and never making use, when I advanced any proposition that might be controversial, of the words *certainly, undoubtedly,* or any others that might give the appearance of being obstinately attached to any opinion. Thus, in the sentences, paragraphs, and pages that follow, if any of the essays laid before you shine a bright light of arrogance and unfettered confidence, whether I am correct or not in a matter, I apologize. If my words were poorly chosen, know that no intellectual pretension was intended.

Alas, it is much easier to grade eggs than lay eggs.
                                        —*Author unknown*

NATIONAL DEFICIT
. . . FDA Labeling

The truth of the matter is that I do watch, rarely fascinated, usually appalled, all too frequently horrified. Most often I avert my eyes from the pablum that poses as entertainment, choosing rather to observe those real-world occurrences of intellectual intrigue or of human humor.

But it was intrigue that drew me to watch your television. Dr. Carl Sagan's *Cosmos* was the program. While my present venue within the very cosmos of which he spoke allows me greater insight—perhaps, better stated, farsight—as to that infinite universe in which the good Earth resides, Dr. Sagan provided a context and calibration to consider our world against all else. It was the latter, the calibration, that caused me to pause when Dr. Sagan lectured that the nearest star to our sun is 4.5 million light-years away. Had he stated that the distance was equal to a hundred ocean voyages between America and England, I would have comprehended the magnitude more surely and quickly, having made many Atlantic crossings under sail and so familiar with this span of miles, the first crossing having been made when I was eighteen, the last sixty-one years later. Moreover, since I well know the magnitude of the number 100, the calculation of the total distance was well within my ken; thus, I would have had a point of reference calibrated by experience. But 4.5 million light-years? Curious reader, it is:

$$186{,}000 \text{ miles} \times 60 \times 60 \times 24 \times 365 \times 4{,}500{,}000$$

I beseech you, wary citizens, do not retrieve your hand-held calculator to perform this multiplication, lest you burn your hand as your clever but overtaxed device melts.

As a million light-years, let alone 4.5 million light-years, is a figure of no relevant experience to almost all Americans, neither, quite apparently, is a trillion dollars. But, fearful reader, I am miserably sorrowful to advise you that it should be.

From what I was able to glean, America's annual deficit is currently a fearsome $1.3 trillion, which, piled on top of past sins . . . excuse me . . . past annual deficits, totals more than $13 trillion.

In all of its enlightened majesty the Food and Drug Administration (FDA) requires that food products be labeled with calories per serving and per package. To assist Americans in understanding fiscal deficits, a Federal Deficit Administration (FDA) should be hastily formed. This new FDA could be staffed by a single energetic bureaucrat possessing a robust calculator. The diligent government employee would, as I trust Congress mandates, divide all deficit numbers by the number of citizens and households in the United States. And all federal programs would be divided by the same two factors. Hence, when your Federal Government announced financial information, it would, as the first FDA required, provide serving information . . . perhaps, as follows:

> *This year we expect a record $1.3 trillion deficit, which, when added to our existing debt, will total $13 trillion. Hence, under FDA labeling criteria, each citizen is responsible for $42,000 of debt, and each household, $113,000 of debt. Accordingly, assuming a 4 percent cost of borrowing, this year we will need a check from each and every American for $1,700 to pay China, Japan, and others for the interest on monies we owe them. Thank you for your time, and God bless America.*

Since I opened this diminutive essay by referencing television, let me return to the great giver of light and noise. For many Americans, television has become both a pacifier and a false voice of self-worth. I came, after much hesitancy, to this conclusion while considering the great Colosseum in Rome. A Colosseum where, for the morbid enjoyment of the masses, humanity was discarded and humans were first degraded, then slain. Many reality TV programs shown today on America's networks likewise degrade humans for the enjoyment of the masses; but, unlike in Rome, the Colosseum is brought to each American's house—no need to exercise by walking to a great amphitheater.

Dear Americans, please—do not sit stationary, as great stuffed animals, in the glow of your television and view those Americans who possess few redeeming attributes, thus taking comfort in your life's station; rather, look to those Americans of productive achievement, in whatever discipline or passion, and strive to better yourself against their mark.

There is much difference in imitating a good man, and counterfeiting him.
—Poor Richard's, *November 1738*

REAL AMERICANS

. . . UNREAL AMERICANS

L ogic would demand that the reciprocal of Real Americans must be Unreal Americans. This notion of real
versus unreal I do profess to comprehend when the subjects are such as literature; a biography versus a novel. But
as to citizens of a country, I am bewildered. Perhaps Josiah

Franklin, my father, affords a perfectly sculptured mold from which to cast the busts of Real Americans.

At the age of twenty-five, with his wife and three children, before I was numbered among them, my father tendered two years of hard-saved money for a hard passage to America, passage on a wooden, creaking ship with more than a score of hopeful families seeking a better life. Better life being greater wages for greater work. After seventy long days and nights of rolling seas, Josiah Franklin set foot in Boston, with him a few coins, a needy family, and hope. Only opportunity stood at the wharf to greet him.

To provide a roof and food for his family, Father did for others that which many believed to be beneath them, so physically strenuous, dirty, and odiferous was this occupation: He became a tallow chandler. In a lean-to attached to his small rented clapboard home, he boiled animal fat and lye to render candles and soaps for the citizens of Boston. This he did for no less than twelve hours each day but Saturday and Sunday. Saturday was for only half Father's work, Sunday was all for God's work.

My father's first wife, Anne, died when Father was thirty-one, but not before she had given him seven children, five of whom lived through infancy. Abiah was my father's second wife, and my mother; together they had ten children, though one died as an infant, another as a toddler. I was the third to last of father's thirteen living children, all of whom were raised in a home twenty feet wide, thirty feet deep, two floors high, with a privy a short walk away. Next to the cots on which we slept was a small factory that produced enough candles and soaps to feed and shelter fifteen family members, and to allow Father to tithe monies to the South Church, where he was a tith-ingman, or, in your words, an elder.

My father's life was simple—not simple as in bland or uninteresting, but simple in the code that governed his life, a code drawn by him from Proverbs 22:29:

> Seest thou a man diligent in his calling, he shall stand before Kings.

But let me return to Americans other than my father and our family.

Real Americans was a term I first heard during the frightful Irish Potato Famine of the late 1840s, half a century after my demise. I was floating through Boston, where I witnessed parades of men protesting the boatloads of arriving Irishmen, these poor souls fleeing the starvation of Ireland. Protesting, these paraders were, that the newly arrived Irish were stealing jobs from Real Americans.

Across King Street I spied a banner that caused me to turn a broad smile. The banner, in large red letters, proclaimed: REAL AMERICANS WERE BORN HERE; THEY DIDN'T COME ON A BOAT. That made me smile when I thought back to two centuries before. I thought of "savages" raising the same banner between two great trees, protesting the arrival of all those Unreal Americans on the *Mayflower* and the hundreds of boats that followed.

Irony set in yet again; indeed, this whole phenomenon of Real versus Unreal Americans is evidently as cyclical and as inevitable as the changing seasons that characterize the passing of a year. Bear witness: Within a few short decades the Irish learned to become Real Americans. They did this by discovering and unmasking those who were not

Real Americans, thus elevating the Irish to the exalted station of Real Americans. As I watched the last spike driven into the Transcontinental Railroad tracks at Promontory, Utah, Irish work crews hurled harsh threats at Chinese laborers, claiming they had stolen the jobs of Real Americans.

Let me return to today's Real Americans versus their "unreal" counterparts. Thwarted I was at first in shaping the profile of today's Real Americans. Perhaps they are the Vietnamese couple who fled to America with the Fall of Saigon, and by working three jobs put both their children through fine schools . . . only to behold a generation later that one child is now a Surgeon, the other a Professor of Chemistry; or perhaps the female army sergeant, the child of a single mother, who is completing her third tour in Iraq and will have earned enough GI benefits to attend college; or perhaps the fourth-generation Iowa farmer who, in his adult life, has never once been in bed when the sun rose and works his two hundred acres while his wife hopes for overtime at a nursing home so she will earn enough in wages for this year's seed corn; or is it, perhaps, the lad who has seen a dozen John Wayne movies a dozen times each, field-dressed a bear after slaying it with a bow and arrow, and drives a rusted-out pickup with a faded bumper sticker proclaiming: AMERICA FIRST, RIGHT OR WRONG.

Obviously, curious reader, Real Americans are only so in the eyes of other Real Americans. But to claim that one American is more genuine than another evokes potential for anger, for discord, for discrimination, for prejudice, and, inevitably, for division. That is not what our America is about. Recall: "United we stand." One of the most potent, most clear essences of America is contained in that immortal line: "All Men Are Created Equal." Let us layer that same notion on not only men, but also on all other citizens of America. "All American Citizens Are Created Equal."[1]

And perhaps I should not speak of our Declaration of Independence and Constitution when I ask that you stand together. No, let me rather speak to a harsh reality. In 1776 we stood together or perished separately . . . that was our battle cry. You too, dear citizens, face a battle: America must pull itself from the velvet-lined rut it has fallen into. Without every shoulder to the wheel, you and your America will not perish; no, a worse fate awaits. Unlike our War of Independence, when if we lost, it was a loss of not achieving greatness, your loss will be that of not *maintaining* greatness. Your defeat will be sorrowful indeed.

---

[1] Perhaps with one exception: If, as the hangman adjusts the noose around your neck, you proclaim loudly, "My only regret is that I have but one life to give for my country," you may then lay claim to the mantle of Real American.

BALLOONS AND FEDERAL BUDGETS

... They Can Only Carry So Much

Three children, gifted to me. Two boys first, then my daughter Sarah. A Sarah addressed as Sally by all who knew her as a friend. But never more than two children in our home on Market Street. My second son, Francis Folger Franklin ... we called him Franky ... taken by

smallpox when he was four. Seven years after Franky
was laid to rest, our daughter's squeals filled my home.
Delightful and sprightly, it was Sally who gave me the most
joy, both as an affectionate child, and later, as a woman
and mother to six. Those six glorious grandchildren who
always had time, questions, and smiles for me, as I always
had answers, limericks, songs, tricks, and love for them.
And from Sally's brood, my favorite grandchild; after two
hundred years I will concede, yes, there was a favorite,
and he was Benny.

In the early summer of 1783 Benny joined me at my
home in Passy, a quaint village only a long walk, or a brief
carriage ride, from Paris. He had been attending school
in Geneva while I had, through the expenditure of much
patience and strategy (more certainly the former than the
latter), helped to negotiate the Provisional Treaty that
ended the Revolutionary War the previous year, though
the final articles of peace were not signed until some con-
siderable time later, after more long months of national
posturing.

With American blood no longer being bartered for liberty, I savored the summer of 1783, with Benny as my guest.
Yet it was the fall of that year that was the most remarkable.
On a cool and clear day we journeyed to Paris with much
anticipation. There, to our delight and wonder, Benny and
I observed Jacques Charles, a Parisian of curious intellect,
ever so patiently pour oil of vitriol on red-hot iron, thus
producing hydrogen that soon expanded and filled a silk
balloon as large as a fair-sized parlor. In time the majestic
balloon rose, then drifted from our view. It carried neither man nor beast aboard. Once touching down on Earth
again some ten miles away, it was attacked by farmers with

passion and fright. Later that fall, November it was, I witnessed the first manned flight: A hot-air balloon ever so slowly lifted two French gentlemen, champagne in hand, high above Paris. At this sight, a sight never seen before, men cheered, women fainted, and I marveled.

Recalling now those attributes, those characteristics, those realities of a balloon's ability to rise, I think again of the troubling news our latest federal budget so recently conveyed to us. Hot-air balloons are not unlike our federal budget. A balloon is only of a certain size and can therefore lift only so many passengers; in this selfsame way, our federal budget can fund only so many federal programs.

If the balloonist wishes to carry more passengers (fund more federal programs), he needs to increase the size of the balloon (increase taxes). If the balloonist wishes to add another passenger (a new federal program) to those already in the basket hanging below the balloon (existing federal programs), he needs to remove an individual (program) from the basket; otherwise, the balloonist must increase the size of the balloon (taxes).

And as certain as the sun rises in the East, as certain as leaves turn brown with fall, all tax increases eventually burden each and every American family. Raise corporate taxes, and corporate executives will not dutifully lower their salaries to maintain their company's profits; rather, the price of a Big Mac, a ride at Disney World, and six pairs of socks in the economy pack, will all drift higher.

My fellow Countrymen and Countrywomen, you may clamor for as many federal programs as you wish. Do so with caution, however; know well that each and every federal program is paid for dearly in the end by us Americans.

For every action, there is an equal and opposite reaction, both in physics and in budgeting.

> *Beware of the little expenses; small leaks will sink the greatest ships.*
>
> —Poor Richard's, January 1745

PREJUDICE

. . . I'M NOT, BUT ALL OF YOU ARE

William Hazlitt became a much-esteemed English essayist and literary critic two decades after I met his father at the University of Glasgow. As an agent of the Pennsylvania Assembly to England, I stole days from my duties to visit Scotland and Ireland. On one such excursion to Edinburgh in 1759, I was honored to meet the most esteemed Adam Smith and David Hume. They and others were then in the midst of creating the Scottish Enlightenment, the intellectual flowering that so distinguished that industrious small nation in my time, which is deserving of much applause and which I was privileged to experience firsthand, however glancingly, by touching its periphery.

Pardon me this slight digression as I tug my recollections back to the theme of this essay, to wit: William Hazlitt famously wrote, "Ignorance is the father of prejudice," a resounding statement that has, over the centuries, quite properly been much repeated in oratory and print. Perhaps his claim that ignorance fathers prejudice is without debate. While not offering debate, permit me to tender for your consideration this proposition: that a foul prejudice may manifest itself also in the offspring of generations down the line; that is, not only in the originating sire's children, but in his grandchild, great-grandchildren, and so on, generation to generation. Prejudice, once firmly rooted, violently resists extirpation. Consider further, if you will, the following:

. Of all those things in a man's life, in his constitution, in his morality, that one thing, that one topic that he cannot speak to, is his own prejudice. Prejudice is not an absolute, is not quantifiable as are ounces to a pint or weights to a scale. Prejudice is a measurement of one man's beliefs against that man's own measuring stick, a measuring stick that is unique to him and resides within his mind: a measuring stick that is uniquely calibrated to that man's life experiences and, of no less weight, to that which he has been taught.

Of the many essays penned by me during my life, many spoke to occurrences that, depending on one's station in the cultural weave then composing the known world, might be perceived as my exercising and venting extreme prejudice. One such essay written by me was "Remarks Concerning the Savages of North America." Certain as I am that for me to address Native Americans as "savages" would undoubtedly now cause most contemporary readers a discomfort, naught of that was true in my unenlightened day, when such sentiments were commonplace, if manifestly inexcusable from the modern vantage point. Quickly, however, and by your leave, permit me to offer for full exegesis the first lines of this oft-misunderstood, and even more frequently mischaracterized, essay:

> *Savages we call them because their manners differ from ours, which we think the perfection of civility; they think the same of theirs.*
> *Perhaps if we could examine the manners of different nations with impartiality, we should find no people so rude as to be without any rules of politeness; nor any so polite as to not have some remains of rudeness.*

In the essay just referenced I later recount a meeting of a distinguished and well-educated Swedish minister and the chiefs of the Susquehanna tribe. The learned minister related to these Native American chiefs many of his religion's truths: Adam and Eve, an apple eaten by them to their peril, a woman untouched by man giving birth to a child, the coming of Christ, water miraculously converted to wine, one loaf multiplied to many, Christ raising himself from the dead, and so on and so forth, numbering the manifold tenets of Christianity.

When the minister concluded his learned recitation, the chiefs responded, in turn, as recorded in my essay of more than two centuries ago:

> *In the beginning, our fathers had only the flesh of animals to subsist on; and if their hunting was unsuccessful, they were starving. Two of our young hunters having killed a deer, made a fire in the woods to broil some parts of it. When they were about to satisfy their hunger, they beheld a beautiful young woman descend from the clouds, and seat herself on that hill which you see yonder among the blue mountains. They said to each other, it is a spirit that perhaps has smelt our broiled venison, and wishes to eat of it; let us offer some to her. They presented her with the tongue; she was pleased with the taste of it, and said, "Your kindness shall be rewarded. Come to this place after thirteen moons, and you shall find something that will be of great benefit in nourishing you and your children to the latest generations." They did so, and to their surprise, found plants they had never seen before, but which, from that ancient time, have been constantly cultivated among us, to our great advantage. Where her right hand had touched the ground, they found maize; where her left hand touched it, they found kidney-beans; and where her backside had sat on it, they found tobacco.*

The Swedish minister, upon hearing this gentle rejoinder, interrupted and disgustedly admonished:

> *What I delivered to you were sacred truths, but what you tell me is mere fable, fiction, and falsehood.*

Neither the chiefs of the Susquehanna nor the Swedish minister were ignorant. Their beliefs of religion sprang forth and took root by each of them having been told by someone, or someones, with a weight of knowledge and credibility, as to the truth of a matter. Hence, I humbly suggest that the acorn of prejudice may well be ignorance, but the growth of the acorn, the spreading of the branches and leaves from one generation to the next, is from father to son, teacher to student, minister to parishioner; that is the cause of prejudice in most men. Then, given that prejudices are passed as knowledge and fact by credible tens of hundreds of speakers to hundreds of hundreds of receptive listeners, the tree of prejudice is not easily cut off at the roots; it must be plucked one leaf at a time.

Now then, let me do what I have just preached no man can do: Let me expound on my prejudices. The truth of the matter is that one may speak only of those prejudices within oneself that in time fester to a boil and make themselves known. Others remain unshown. In my life, slavery was a prejudice often justified by economic need, justified by considering those most undesirable attributes laid upon slaves by their masters as attributes from the womb, and justified by no remedy to undo what had been done.

In time my once-firm stance toward slavery ever so slowly turned from conviction to a wobbly uncertainty. I owned slaves, they served me, they did my bidding. My paper, the *Pennsylvania Gazette*, printed advertisements for the sale of slaves. I spoke poorly of their nature. In time, much time, after observing black children in a Philadelphia school that I had assisted others in establishing for the offspring of slaves, I wrote:

I was on the whole much pleased, and from what I then saw have conceived a higher opinion of the natural capacities of the black race than I had ever before entertained. Their apprehension seems as quick, their memory as strong, and their docility in every respect equal to that of white children. You will wonder perhaps that I should ever doubt it, and I will not undertake to justify all my prejudices.

There was one prejudice of mine, and I think of all of the Founding Fathers, that remained below our skins, never showing itself as a boil. A prejudice that was handed, one to another, from our fathers, their fathers, and all before. A prejudice of an arbitrary belief that was never spoken of at the Constitutional Convention. A prejudice that because it was not obvious, as a black man or a red man with their differences of color and culture, did not boil to the surface of our skin and erupt in an epiphany of remorse. But a prejudice that when declared with words carefully and poignantly chosen to unmask the absurdity of the matter, is shown to be the most arbitrary of all prejudices. Such words as follows: I and the other Founding Fathers felt no need, no passion, no equity in allowing those American citizens with internal reproductive organs the right to vote; rather, this most cherished privilege to cast a vote was only for those enlightened Americans with external reproductive organs.

THE RISE AND FALL OF NATIONS

... WHY LIONS DON'T CARRY WALLETS

Since I took my final leave that warm April evening in 1790, the greatest application of my time has been watching and listening to my fellow Americans in our America. Curiosity has, however, taken me to other lands;

perhaps, better stated, more than curiosity, it was a concern for our nation's well-being that took me abroad.

In the early fall of 1918, near the conclusion of the Great War, I hovered over those scarred green fields surrounding Jonville; I confess that I turned away when I saw the American blood of then Colonel George S. Patton's infantry soaking French soil. Again in the 1940s I repaired to Europe, there to witness a far greater War, a War that produced seventy million deaths and wrapped the entire Earth in a shroud of sorrow. And again I saw the blood of now General Patton's troops on foreign soil, first in Sicily, then in France, and finally in Germany.

I was in England for much of the year 1944; it was the spring of that year when I drifted to Cambridge University, its colleges not visited by me for close to two centuries. More precisely, the year I had last visited Cambridge was 1758, when I last saw the flat-bottomed boats on the River Cam. These boats were being poled along, though in England they called it "punting"; the black-robed students of Cambridge stood astern and punted these shallow boats along the Cam, under the beautiful ancient stone bridges beside the green banks and emerald lawns that were grass place mats to the most stunning examples of English Gothic architecture in all the world.

But back to 1758; that year Professor Hadley and I conducted an experiment with ether and a bellows, demonstrating the cooling power of evaporation. For most of an hour the good professor and I would alternately place the ball of a thermometer in ether and then blow on it with vigor by using a bellows such as blacksmiths employ. Even though it was May . . . I believe it was . . . soon the temperature dropped below the freezing point and a thin coat of ice began to cover the ball. By the end of an hour of labor, more than a quarter of an inch of ice covered the lower half of the thermometer. I beg your pardon, I digressed from this essay's topic; the older I am, the more frequent the digressions.

Let me return to my most recent visit in 1944 to Cambridge, England, not Massachusetts. Few differences I saw after so long; perhaps the most telling were the noises, one sound of the past shoved away by another. No longer the steady beat of iron-rimmed coach and wagon wheels against those canals of hard cobblestones which crisscrossed among the colleges, homes, and shops of Cambridge. Only silent rubber-clad spinning disks of bikes and automobiles on cobblestones, conveying commerce and impatient people.

But a new noise, a new sound, was seeping from open windows and doors. Radios that could speak, sing, and play music addressed me most everywhere I drifted, whether I paid them a mind or not. Another difference: the faces, professors and students—no familiar faces, no old friends. I knew this would be so, but still I looked with anticipation.

Slowly, from college to college I moved. At each I paused, some for hours, others a brief stay. Most things I remembered, and most things were the same: stone-walled facades, some crumbling and sagging; great oak doors guarding the colleges, some with reliefs that I recollected; stained-glass windows no less perfect and pleasing to the eye than before; and magnificent, yes, magnificent libraries, the same as long ago.

It was while I lingered at Christ's College, where Charles Darwin's grandson had just relinquished his esteemed role as Master of the College, that my casual eavesdropping caused my bones to turn cold . . . a poor figure of speech, indeed, given my present wispy state of being. In the tomb-quiet library of Christ's College I spied a strange sight. An American wearing the scholarly robes of U.S. Army khaki leaned over a table conning hard a file box of papers, some of which were spread before him. I drifted over to his side. He was an air corps pilot. Later I learned he had force-landed his fighter at nearby Duxford Airfield. I peered over his shoulder to see what papers he was studying with such concentration. Then I understood.

The young army lieutenant was reading letters from no less a scholarly god than Charles Darwin. Peering closer, I discerned that they were letters sent from the HMS *Beagle* during her five-year exploration of the South Pacific, letters held in the library for the scholars of Christ's College to read and ponder. Letters that hinted of Darwin's first tentative conclusions drawn from his observations of the tortoise and finch populations of the Galapagos Islands— conclusions that led to his anti-Christ Theory of Organic Evolution: Natural Selection.

So engrossed were Warren—that was the name of the American serviceman—and I with Darwin's handwritten papers that shadows became long with no notice taken by either of us. In time a young man broke our trance by asking Warren if all was in order. The interruptor was Giles, a Professor of Biology as well as a fellow of Christ's College. He had graciously allowed the young American lieutenant to peruse Darwin's correspondence upon learning that Warren's father was an American Professor of Biology who revered Darwin. Giles, after confirming that Warren had completed paying homage to Darwin, in a tone more like an order than a suggestion, asked him to join him for the evening meal. Warren accepted his kind offer, and I followed.

The dinner was laid in the refectory at Christ's College, in a dark room of darker woods. Even though Mr. Edison's electric lights hung from the ceiling, only candles roosting on a long oak table fought the darkness. In the flickering yellow candlelight many still faces peered down, ponderous portraits of academia's finest, frowning from the walls. One of which I had debated successfully, or at least I thought successfully at the time, so long ago.

After dining on typical British fare of starches and fatty meat—of course I did not partake—Giles shoved and pulled Warren through a premise I'd never before contemplated . . . lest I become weak of spirit and shorn of all hope. He transposed Darwin's theory of natural selection from animal and plant species to human cultures and nations.

For the young professor it was no less a certitude that Darwin's theory of evolution explained man's existence than his certitude of the validity of Newton's observations regarding fruit and gravity: Men evolved; gravity pulled downward. Giles explained to Warren, as an indisputable fact, that civilizations, and later in the history of our planet, nations, rise and then fall as the fittest nation becomes less fit.

Warren, whose speech and selection of words attested that he was truly a learned citizen of America, questioned Giles's proclamation. He speculated that if it was true that the fittest species tended to remain the fittest, why would not the fittest nation likewise hold fast to its dominant place in the world ranking? Giles's answer gave me pause. Mankind, he argued, is a unique species. And it is mankind that forms each nation. Warren's furrowed brow elicited further explanation. The Spanish, Giles lectured, had been prominent in the 1400s and 1500s. They were a global power in the world as then constituted. As a nation they had succeeded. Boats riding low with gold from the New World to Madrid confirmed their exalted status among States. In time, Giles propositioned, Spain, or, more fairly stated, the people of Spain, applied their wealth not to expand, but to enjoy life, paying others to do both their bidding and their work. As a people, as a nation, they became lazy or, perhaps a more generous phrasing, they became less industrious. Giles concluded by stating that while Spain was in decline, it was England that was striving the most diligently in the 1600s and 1700s; by the conclusion of the 1800s, Britannia ruled the waves, not Spain.

To validate his theory by comparing the rise and fall of nations to the survival of the fittest animal and plant species, Giles asked that Warren consider the lion, the long-proclaimed King of the Jungle, with no other wild animal challenging its dominance. Imagine, he said, what would happen if the lion killed more game than it needed for survival. Imagine as well that African animals had money that they freely exchanged. Lions could sell the excess meat from their kills and, if they wished, save a portion of the money they received. Some future generation of lions might use this stored wealth of their ancestor lions to pay leopards to hunt and provide meat for them, rather than being bothered to themselves stalk gazelles beneath the blazing African sun. In time these lions, who paid others to hunt for them, would become fat and less agile, not fleet of paw and firm of flank. Leopards, still being lean and cunning, and noting the lions' laziness, might tire of hunting as paid servants of the lions and decide instead to eat the flabby, slow, easy-to-kill lions.

Laziness travels so slowly, that poverty overtakes.
—Poor Richard's, *September 1756*

After a few moments of reflection, Warren asked if Great Britain would decline. "For certain" was Giles's quick and rigid answer, adding that Winston Churchill was spot-on in the fall of 1940 when he declared the Battle of Britain to be England's finest hour. Not only the epic grandeur of the event made it Britain's finest hour, Giles stated, but the subsequent decline of Great Britain as the world's greatest power would mark the Battle of Britain as the clear high-water mark for the British Empire.

After cordials and an unstructured discussion of classical music that held little interest for me . . . the classical music held no interest, otherwise for the cordials . . . Warren jibbed and tacked Giles into a continued discussion of the evolutionary path of nations. He asked what nation would be the next dominant. Giles quickly replied, "The United States." Warren then questioned whether America would tumble from a position of dominance once it was attained. For a few silent moments Giles stared at Warren as if he had asked Newton whether the apple would rise or fall in its journey from the tree. "Of course," he replied, "and it will decline faster than England."

Before Warren could ask why so, as I knew he would, his obvious intellect being both curious and challenging, Giles put forth the reason: "The speed of commerce has increased over the centuries and will continue to increase. Just as it took a country with a fleet of steamships less time to move commerce than a nation with a fleet of sailing ships, new technologies will provide for a relentless compression of time, thus accelerating a nation's ability to move from have-not to have . . . to displace the dominant. "Hence," Giles stated while pouring Warren another cordial, "America, once attaining the position of the World's Greatest Nation, will decline to a lesser status more rapidly than any other of the previous Greatest Nations of our planet."

RELIGIONS, WINDOWS TO GOD

...HEATHENS PEER THROUGH CIRCULAR WINDOWS

One month before I departed your Earth, I knew the last page of my well-worn book was near. It so happened that my good friend, the Reverend Ezra Stiles of Yale, the President of that great College, asked whether I had accepted Jesus as my savior. As your contemporary jargon would have it, I punted. To the good Reverend I wrote that Jesus offered unto man the most worthy structure of morals the world had ever seen, or would likely ever see. I did not equivocate. On whether Jesus was divine I proffered these uncertain thoughts: "I have some doubts as to his divinity; though it is a question I do not dogmatize upon, having never studied it, and think it needless to busy myself with it now, when I expect soon an opportunity of knowing the truth with less trouble." Again, as you would say, "That was then and this is now."

My present status and venue allow me to address you on this subject of religion with a certain perspective and credibility that none of you yet possess. I will neither speak of Jesus as the Son of God, nor speak of God, but for you, most courteous and curious reader, I will identify that which is the holiest and most sacred of those religions practiced on our good Earth. But first, a short discourse containing a parable crafted to convey the truth of the matter.

Talk against religion is unchaining a tiger; the beast let loose may devour his keeper.
—Poor Richard's, *September 1751*

I ask that you imagine, in the beginning of our world, that all of mankind had lived together in a large dark room with no windows or portals. Outside, the sun, with its life-giving warmth and light, shone brightly, but not on cloistered mankind. In time religions within the dark room sprang forth to help mankind see and feel the sun's golden glow. Each religion, within the confines of this dark room, constructed its own unique window, thus allowing its followers to bask in a Godly life of light and warmth. While each window, each religion, was unique, they all let in the sun's blessing of light.

The window built by the Quakers was square with no glass, only shutters at its sides to hold back the night's coldness. Presbyterians gathered and prayed before a large window with six clear panes of leaded glass, constructed by their most holy ministers. Another window constructed by the Jews took the shape of a six-pointed star. Followers of the Vatican knelt before an arched window of many multicolored panes that together depicted Mary, Mother of God, while Muslims flocked to the crescent moon and star window.

Although each window was different from any other, they all admitted the sun's holy grace; and the light flowing through each window onto that window's religious believers in no way diminished the light flowing through the other windows onto the believers of the other religions. The sun's rays unfailingly shone bright and full on all believers who gathered before a particular religion's window, a window of their own choosing.

If the leaders of one religion beseeched others to leave their religion's window and instead feel the sun's warmth through their own religion's window, by tendering whatever argument or logic—"Our window is not distorted by colored glass"—so be it. But over time such solicitation empowered the Devil to play his hand. Manifestly it is the Devil's work when pious leaders of one religion teach that only their window offers the true light and warmth, the True God, and, further teach that to view the sun through any window other than theirs is wrong, and thereby diminishes and insults the light and warmth that flows through their one true window.

But that, I fear, represents not the worst of treachery in the name of religion. For reasons and motives comprising varying portions of insecurity, self-importance, greed, dogmatic disputation, ignorance, lack of stature, or sexual confusion, the Devil's most trusted disciples proclaim, while speaking as the anointed leaders of their religion, and usually in a most unseemly, animal-like rant—if animals could speak, they would be truly offended—that worshippers enjoying the warmth and light of the sun through a window other than their own should be slain and their untrue window destroyed.

Pious leaders speaking for God drive more to atheism than the Devil.
—Poorer Richard's America, *September 2010*

So then, dear reader, which religion on Earth speaks of the True God and is most righteous? The answer is self-evident. It is the religion that does not claim it stands above any other religion that teaches all mankind should love one another.

DEMOCRACY
. . . DIRT FLOORS, NO; WOOD FLOORS, YES

Feel uneasy I do when I listen to Americans of high position lecturing that America must forthwith deliver democracy to other nations, as if we were dispatching a great sailing ship with bales of cotton to England.

We humans have primary needs: food, shelter, loving family. Food trumps all other wants, followed by shelter for man and his family. But that is not what my friend Thomas Paine offered. Did you know that he came ever so close to being guillotined by the French? Let me return to my essay's theme; Thomas Paine's *Common Sense* of 1776 argued for the separation of the Colonies from the King, and set forth a call to create a nation of democracy. *Common Sense*, a pamphlet of over forty pages, was distributed throughout the Colonies to colonists who enjoyed, as you would say, "a standard of living" not different from farmers and shopkeepers in England. By 1776 most American colonists had their primary needs met; hence, they had the energy, both physical and emotional, to ponder a change in who was to rule them and by which manner of government.

Now, consider if *Common Sense* had been distributed 160 years earlier to the Jamestown colonists—colonists who were dying from disease, starvation, and attacks by "savages." *Common Sense* pamphlets would have been wadded into their coats as down, or perhaps used as kindling. By 1776, the colonists had wood floors in their homes, while in 1610, the Jamestown colonists lived their meager lives in dirt-floored huts.

Do not, dear Americans, attempt to deliver democracy unto those nations where people are hungry, fearful, and live their meager lives on dirt floors. More compelling wants consume their energies, and someone responding to such wants can easily outbid those Americans who tender a nebulous democracy of no substance to a nation of hungry and fearful citizens.

*Sweet cakes must be baked in family ovens; they
cannot be delivered from afar.*
　　　　　　　—Poorer Richard's America, *September 2010*

And, if I might be permitted, since I was there—being
bitten by horseflies as beads of sweat rolled down my
forehead and in front of my ears, as they were being
most offended by the sounds of Mr. Sherman picking his
teeth (of course, to speak ill of another is not my wont,
and in his defense, Roger was a brilliant Mayor of New
Haven and a leading mathematician, who, in a few brief
years, began to manufacture splendid astronomical calculations for almanacks, and, as you all well know, any man
affiliated with the making of almanacks justly commands
a large piece of my heart)—but let me rejoin and now speak
of that majestic document.

As I do trust that you most likely know, our Declaration
of Independence was drafted and signed in the summer
of 1776 in my Philadelphia. It was a few brief weeks in
preparation, a few long years in coming. We members of
the Continental Congress did not wish, at first, to break
with England; and, yes, it was our England back then; as
we were Americans in the Colonies, also we were English.
Proud English; but in time, less so. But do know that the
"in time" was not of a brief duration. For years we struggled, I struggled, to weave a mesh of understanding and
arrangements by which we, the Colonies and England,
could prosper and live harmoniously in a world of mutual
respect. Or, in your words, as you so succinctly phrase it
today, "We did our best to make it work."

And please know that between 1757 and 1775, I spent no less than fifteen years in England representing the Colonies' interests while attempting to negotiate a peaceful settlement between America and England. Only in March of 1775, when I returned to Philadelphia, did I acquiesce to emotions of bitterness toward England. As I wrote an old friend, an English friend, a friend who had served in the House of Commons:

> Mr. Stratham,
>   You are a member of Parliament, and one of that majority which has doomed my country to destruction. You have begun to burn our towns and murder our people. Look upon your hands! They are stained with the blood of your relations! You and I were long friends; you are now my enemy, and I am
>
>   Yours,
>   B. Franklin

The truth of the matter is that never did I post the letter. Putting the words to paper served its purpose, my hostile emotions drained, with no friendships mortally wounded.

So then, let me return to the horseflies; they resided comfortably in the stable below the dripping-hot room where a committee of five selected from the Continental Congress labored, by ever so carefully crafting each phrase, to memorialize America's Declaration of Independence. This committee of five was Mr. Jefferson, Mr. Adams, Mr. Sherman, Mr. Livingston, and a seventy-year-old printer. As I pray that you know, Thomas Jefferson, that young, well-read gentleman from Virginia, composed the first draft. I will not labor you with a full description of the drafting and redrafting. I will, though, say that I deleted Mr. Jefferson's "sacred and undeniable" and replaced these three words with one hyphenated word, thus: "we hold these truths to be *self-evident.*"

On July 2, the Continental Congress voted for independence. Our Declaration of Independence, the parchment copy not signed until August 2, was dated July 4, 1776.

My point by now, I trust, is as loud and clear as was the tolling of the Liberty Bell. Know well that no one brought democracy to our America. Rather, by action that summer of 1776, we began a fight, a fight of long, hard years, to win our democracy as the most magnificent spoil of war to the victor.

A PLEASANT NIGHT'S SLEEP

. . . OR, UNCONTROLLED CRYING AND DIARRHEA

A most casual observation of your habits and tendencies reveals that most Americans seek to make better their body and mind by the swallowing of all sizes and shapes of pills. As soldiers standing in formation, there are rows and rows of medicines in your chemistry shops . . . pardon, pharmacies; one for any discomfort, malady, or inconvenience: can't sleep, can't wake, hyperactive, no energy, depressed, wish to gain weight, wish to lose weight, indigestion, sore muscles, don't want to conceive, can't procreate; hundreds of medications offered for any occasion.

If I might, permit me to lay before you a portion of a letter written by me 250 years ago regarding how best to acquire a restful sleep, a restful night's sleep being a reliable antidote to, and remedy for, many ailments, real and imagined:

> As a great part of our life is spent in sleep, during which we have sometimes pleasant and sometimes painful dreams, it becomes of some consequence to obtain the one kind and avoid the other; for whether real or imaginary, pain is pain and pleasure is pleasure. If we can sleep without dreaming, it is well that painful dreams are avoided. If, while we sleep, we can have any pleasant dreams, it is, as the French say, autant de gagné, so much added to the pleasure of life.
>
> To this end it is, in the first place, necessary to be careful in preserving health by due exercise and great temperance; for in sickness the imagination is disturbed, and disagreeable, sometimes terrible, ideas are apt to present themselves. Exercise should precede meals, not immediately follow them; the first promotes, the latter, unless moderate, obstructs digestion. If, after exercise, we feed sparingly, the digestion will be easy and good, the body lightsome, the temper cheerful, and all the animal functions performed agreeably. Sleep, when it follows, will be natural and undisturbed, while indolence, with full feeding, occasions nightmares and horrors inexpressible; we fall from precipices, are assaulted by wild beasts, murderers, and demons,

and experience every variety of distress. Observe, however, that the quantities of food and exercise are relative things; those who move much may, and indeed ought to, eat more; those who use little exercise should eat little. In general, mankind, since the improvement of cookery, eat about twice as much as nature requires. Suppers are not bad if we have not dined; but restless nights follow hearty suppers after full dinners.

When you are awakened and find you cannot easily sleep again, get out of bed, beat with at least twenty shakes, then throw the bed open and leave it to cool; in the meanwhile walk about your chamber. When you begin to feel the cold air unpleasant, then return to your bed and you will soon fall asleep, and your sleep will be sweet and pleasant. All the scenes presented to your fancy will be, too, of the pleasing kind. I am often as agreeably entertained with them as by the scenery of an opera. If you happen to be too indolent to get out of bed, you may, instead of it, lift up your bedclothes with one arm and leg, so as to draw in a good deal of fresh air, and by letting them fall force it out again. This repeated twenty times will so clear them of the perspirable matter they have imbibed as to permit your sleeping well for some time afterward. But this latter method is not equal to the former.

One or two observations will conclude this little piece. Care must be taken, when you lie down, to dispose your pillow so as to suit your manner of placing your head and to be perfectly easy; then place your limbs so as not to bear inconveniently hard upon one another, as, for instance, the joints of your ankles; for though a bad position may at first give but little pain and be hardly noticed, yet a continuance will render it less tolerable, and the uneasiness may *come on while you are asleep and disturb your imagination. These are the rules of the art. But though they will generally prove effectual in producing the end intended, there is a case in which the most punctual observance of them will be totally fruitless. I need not mention the case to you, my dear friend; but my account of the art would be imperfect without it. The case is when the person who desires to have pleasant dreams has not taken care to preserve, what is necessary above all things, A GOOD CONSCIENCE.*

Alternatively, fretful sleeper, today you may acquire, for a few coins lifted from your purse, sleeping medication prescribed by a Doctor well versed on today's commercial pharmaceuticals; well versed by a drug manufacturer's sales representative . . . most often a young lass with taut Ligaments of Cooper suspending resplendent mammary glands. As printed on the medicine's container, such sleeping medications only having the following possible side effects: headaches, aggressive behavior, confusion, memory loss, hallucinations, depression, suicidal thoughts, anxiety, uncontrolled crying, nausea, vomiting, diarrhea, and swelling of the throat.

Whence such side effects, one wonders? It is, however, upon label inspection, not difficult to imagine their source in light of the medication's composition: a typical sleeping pill being a brew of colloidal silicon dioxide, hypromellose, lactose monohydrate, magnesium stearate, microcrystalline cellulose, polyethylene glycol, potassium bitartrate, red ferric oxide, sodium starch glycolate, and titanium dioxide. What! No ground rat's tail?

Perhaps, one might consider my long-ago advice: Fluff your pillow well.

9

AMERICA'S GREATEST GENERATION

. . . Perhaps Less So, Perhaps More So

Uncomfortable I am in suggesting, even in the most gentle of manner, that the underlying premise of Mr. Brokaw's best-seller, *The Greatest Generation*, while not flawed, may not be of such a certitude that those possessed with an open mind might consider alternatives and reflect, for a few brief moments, on other generations that struggled mightily.

The spine of Mr. Brokaw's premise being that those Americans who fought in World War II, and those who labored heroic hours in the fields and factories of America during those same years, combined to be the greatest generation of Americans ever. While epic in proportion, World War II was a challenge of little controversy for Americans. Rather, the challenge had an absolute clarity of purpose: Train, feed, arm, and transport a few million soldiers, sailors, marines, and airmen. There was no gut-tearing national debate as to what should be done. Japan had attacked America's Pacific Fleet; flotillas of German U-boats were sinking Atlantic shipping. There was a national and an individual commitment as to what America and Americans should do, what we had to do. Declare war. Win war.

Of all American generations, your Tom bestowed "greatest" on one that he knew. "Neighbors always seemed to be going to or coming home from the war. My grandfather followed the war's progress in *Time* magazine and on his map." From Tom's perspective, they were the greatest. And, from any American's perspective, they were truly great. But, dear reader, I have seen, firsthand, earlier generations of Americans, generations that fought in other conflicts, and in doing so suffered agonies not visited on Tom's Greatest Generation.

Our American Revolutionary War and Civil War were not a response to foreign aggressors. These wars were the culmination of years of internal friction, debate, and self-doubt. Make no mistake: to fight our British cousins tore at our souls. And to join the fight meant leaving our farms and shops behind, with wives and children fending for themselves. Likewise, ninety years later, Americans weren't asked to fight foreigners who threatened their lands. Sons, husbands, and fathers in Pennsylvania, Massachusetts, Ohio, Illinois, and other northern states were asked to abandon their families to bear arms against other Americans for a cause. A cause that, no matter how noble and just, was of no consequence to their well-being.

> *There have been as great souls unknown to fame as any of the most famous.*
> —Poor Richard's, July 1734

Those generations who fought in America's wars were not alone in suffering great sacrifices. Consider the first generation of Americans, those at Jamestown, whose reward for surviving a cruel ocean crossing in sixty-foot boats was a winter of death by disease and starvation. But enough of the long past; permit me to readdress Mr. Brokaw's generation of great Americans.

With an equivocation that would render any of your elected officials proud, let me assume the opposing side of the argument I just tendered—the argument that casts the smallest shadow of a doubt on the World War II generation being declared The Greatest Generation. There was another attribute they had that was not written of by Mr. Brokaw: an attribute of restraint.

For a few brief years, between 1945 and 1949, America possessed an ability and a power that no man, ruler, or nation had possessed for the thousands of years before; a power that for Alexander the Great, Genghis Khan, Attila the Hun, Cyrus the Great, and Charlemagne consumed their lives, and cost the lives of millions, in a futile attempt to attain: America had the power to rule the world.

With the surrender of Germany and Japan in 1945, the industrial nations of the world were either crushed in defeat or bankrupt in victory. Only our America remained victorious and financially robust. Moreover, only America possessed the atomic bomb and a fleet of hundreds of B-29s that could deliver ultimate devastation to any point in the world. But the Greatest Generation, or, more precisely, those American leaders elected by the Greatest Generation, did not use America's singular and omnipotent power to threaten or sway other nations of the world. Rather, they applied America's fiscal might to rebuild many war-ravaged nations . . . including those that had sought to destroy us. America, in all its nobleness, demonstrated both a restraint of power and a willingness to reconstitute its foes that truly marked this nation as The Greatest.

REPUBLICANS AND DEMOCRATS

. . . HONKERS AND QUACKERS

There would be much mirth to the matter if it were not so tragic; I speak of your two political parties. I speak of the Republicans and the Democrats. By your leave, for this essay I will border my thoughts to Congress. A Congress that resides in that great domed Capitol. A dome that should, perhaps, be yanked from its base, turned slowly and carefully upside down, and then set gently back on its foundation. Having done so, the Capitol would be a great white cauldron. A cauldron to hold the self-importance, self-interest, hypocrisy, duplicity, insecurity, incompetence, and those other attributes that many Americans now accept as the hallmark of their Congress. A Congress that was so hopefully conceived long ago to be that wondrous body of "the people's representatives doing the people's work."

And again, by your leave, let me not refer to America's two parties as Republicans and Democrats, lest I risk offending the spirits of past members of those parties whose foremost intents and energies were never but for America and America's citizens. Honest differences existed, debates were held, many heated; but there was a civility to the matter. There was acknowledgment, in words and actions, that honest differences between reasonable and knowledgeable parties might legitimately exist. So then, let me refer to your two political parties as the Geese and the Ducks; a moment of reflection please . . . no, more-telling names spring to mind. Let them be known henceforth as the Honkers and the Quackers.

> *Great talkers, little doers.*
> —Poor Richard's, *April 1733*

Schoolboys taunting one another in front of the Boston Grammar School when I was a young lad; nothing more clearly comes to mind as I listen to your Honkers and Quackers address one another. If these taunts were cloistered, held within the confines of our Capitol, only their ears would be offended. But these new boys, these Honkers and Quackers, stand before the media, media with twenty-four-hour-a-day coverage of two hours of news worthy of human intellect . . . "We interrupt this program to bring you live aerial coverage of a starlet, of both reclusive talent and intellect, being taken from her home to jail for a driving violation." With their well-draped clothes and coiffed hair, these representatives of the people stand before the national media as cockatoos, repeating their party's most bizarre, inaccurate, and self-serving statements that for most Americans sadly reconfirm what they so fearfully comprehend: Congress is as a great team of horses, some harnessed as they should be, head-to-tail, others head-to-head while others tail-to-tail, thus ensuring that Congress, while dropping great mounds of horse manure, makes scant progress, exhibits little sense, and achieves only the slightest movement.

In my letter of 1784 to Benjamin Vaughan, I reluctantly wrote:

> We assemble parliaments and councils to have the benefit of their collective wisdom; but we necessarily have, at the same time, the inconvenience of their collected passions, prejudices, and private interests.

When not demonizing the opposition, many of the Honkers and Quackers peck for corn; this pecking is usually done at fund-raisers, held one after another in an endless procession. Such elaborate fund-raisers are orchestrated by hundreds of Washington Lobbyists who, for wondrous fees bestowed upon them by corporate clients, guide these clients to our Capitol, where they gently stroke the feathers of the Honkers and Quackers. Some stroke so softly and frequently that a Honker or a Quacker will forsake his congressional nest to roost in the executive offices of a corporation, thus receiving much corn for favors past and considerations to come, such considerations to be extracted from former congressional colleagues.

Still other Honkers and Quackers are the most clever of all. When hunting season opens for geese, such Honkers begin to quack, thus, by sound, signaling to one and all that they are ducks. As duck-hunting season approaches, they once again honk a goose's honk. Their counterparts among the Quackers merely reverse this oh-so-clever trick.

Please know that my remarks that have so despairingly bruised your Congress are not void of an awareness of those issues of emotion and significance presently before this august body. But is that not what Congress is about: difficult choices and stinging compromises? And, sirs and ladies, greater issues of emotion and weight have been long ago before this nation. Recall the great constitutional debate as to whether representatives in Congress would be appointed equally by state or by population, apportioned by the numbers of citizens within each state. Witness, with a permission I trust you favorably grant, those words below conveyed by me to other members of the Constitutional Convention, when discussion flowed toward discourse and I feared a feckless stalemate.

It has given me great pleasure to observe that till this point, the proportion of representation, came before us, our debates were carried on with great coolness and temper. If anything of a contrary kind has on this occasion appeared, I hope it will not be repeated; for we are sent hither to consult, not to contend, with each other, and declarations of a fixed opinion, and of determined resolution never to change it, neither enlighten nor convince us. Positiveness and warmth on one side naturally beget like on the other, and tend to create and augment discord and division in a great concern, wherein harmony and union are extremely necessary to give weight to our counsels and render them effectual in promoting and securing the common good.

No less a document than the estimable Constitution of our Great United States was neither easily, nor readily, taken to the bosom of each of its signers. Grave doubt persisted for many members of the Convention as our looming Constitution was drafted and redrafted; many state representatives, in order to reach an agreement, had to forfeit principles that, when debate began, were held inviolate. Again, with your leave, I humbly share with you my speech of September 17, 1787, beseeching conciliation and harmony among those representatives of the Constitutional Convention . . . the Constitution that was unanimously approved the following day.

I confess that I do not entirely approve of this Constitution at present. But, Sir, I am not sure I shall never approve it; for, having lived long, I have experienced many instances of being obliged, by better information or fuller consideration, to change my opinions even on important subjects, which I thought right but found to be otherwise. It is therefore that, the older I grow, the more apt I am to doubt my own judgment . . .

Thus I consent, Sir, to this Constitution, because I expect no better and because I am not sure that it is not the best. The opinions I have had of its errors I sacrifice to the public good. I have never whispered a syllable of them abroad. Within these walls they were born, and here they shall die. If every one of us, in returning to our constituents, were to report the objections he has had to it and endeavor to gain partisans in support of them, we might prevent its being generally received . . . I hope, therefore, for our own sakes as a part of the people, and for the sake of our posterity, that we shall act heartily and unanimously in recommending this Constitution, wherever our influence may extend, and turn our future thoughts and endeavors to the means of having it well administered.

On the whole, Sir, I cannot help expressing a wish that every member of the convention who may still have objections to it would, with me, on this occasion doubt a little of his own infallibility and, to make manifest our unanimity, put his name to the instrument.

Henceforth no more schoolboy taunts and jibes by me; rather, let me address today's Republicans and Democrats in a sentimental and heartfelt manner: I would humbly, hopefully, prayerfully request that for America's sake, you discard those broad-brushstroke statements damning each other and each other's convictions, whether these damning statements be proffered directly or by surrogates. No Americans holding public office are Nazis . . . to imply such a thing is to flaunt an inexcusable ignorance of the greatest stain on all humanity. Never have Americans been so sick or cruel. Neither are Americans ever heartless; and no Americans wish grief to befall other Americans. So, cease and desist. Please.

> *He that sows thorns, should never go barefoot.*
> —Poor Richard's, *August 1756*

As I bring this essay to a conclusion, I must tender my most sincere apologies; for I have, in those paragraphs written above, exercised a grievous prejudice, such prejudice being the application of certain traits and characteristics of a few to the many. Within today's Congress there are ever so many gentlemen and ladies who adhere to those principles of our democracy's administration as laid forth that hot and so humid summer of our Constitutional Convention. To these senators and representatives I apologize, but! Silence is not golden if the deck is rotting beneath your feet. Speak up. You are not a passenger on a sailing vessel as it tacks toward a rocky shoal. You are the crew of this great ship, a ship with America's hopes and future belowdecks. Speak up. Speak up loudly. Pound your fist.

> *The first mistake in public business is the going into it.*
> —Poor Richard's, *July 1758*

THE MOMENT OF CONCEPTION

. . . SOONER THAN YOU MAY THINK

Both intrigued and perplexed I am with your great national debates: global warming, same-sex marriages, immigration, cable versus satellite, deficit spending, right-to-life versus pro-choice. At times the latter issue generates the most passionate discourse; among the scarred combatants is one of the many heated disagreements: At which very instant does life begin? At what time does that mystical moment of conception occur? After that magical moment, any action taken to thwart the birth of a wailing ball of humanity is thus deemed by many to be an offense to the Supreme Being.

After much study of the matter, after much observation . . . truly, I averted my eyes as necessary to protect the sanctity of the marriage bed . . . and after much reflection, I came to know the precise moment of conception. When, in the soft glow of a candle, the young lass, with adoring eyes, ever so close to the broad-shouldered lad, with her warm breath on his, as that lad, with a single, but ever-so-powerful stroke, pulls the cork from the second bottle of Madeira, to interrupt them from that moment on is to thwart conception, and thus offend the grand design of the Supreme Being.

> *When the wine enters, out goes the reason.*
> —Poor Richard's, *February 1755*

THE RICH SHOULD PAY
THEIR FAIR SHARE
. . . Many Do

Permit me to address a turbulent tax topic that causes me a grimace. This grimace is brought forth by the familiar chant of more than a few candidates seeking votes: "The rich should pay their fair share." To explain my twisting-bowel grimace, let me recount my first forty-two years on our good Earth—this done not to sway your sympathies to kindness, but to shine a light on a bias I perceive in America.

My childhood was one consisting of hard work, frugality, and attendance; attendance to worship at the South Church across from my father's clapboard house on High and Milk streets in lively Boston. One of God's kindnesses is that a child does not know of those things and privileges missed by not being of a better station in life; thus, a youthful life is not burdened with a covetousness of things not held. As a young lad my life was most pleasant. Two of the most enjoyable adventures were larks of swimming in the Charles River and reading. Yes, reading was an adventure. It took me places my feet could never tread, and my mind to experiences never savored. But as with every child in our home, much of my time was filled with the trade that paid our keep. An hour before school each day, and no fewer than two hours after school, I toiled beside my father to make candles and soaps. Only when I had all my labors complete would Mother allow me to ride my bike, and then, only if I wore a helmet . . . sorry, but I do so enjoy a fanciful untruth delivered with a twinkle.

When I was but ten I began full-time work for my father; there were no more days for me at Boston Grammar School under the squinting gray eyes of Mr. Brownwell. Strange, is it not, this feat of memory; names of uncles and aunts we forget, teachers never. For my father, from boiling-hot tubs of fat I skimmed tallow, then poured this hot, stinking—yes, stinking!—essence of cow fat into candle molds; before the odiferous tallow congealed, I placed trimmed wicks in each mold, thus making a serviceable candle. Perhaps this routine offers a mentally stimulating task for some of God's creatures, but not for man, nor boy.

After two years of skimming and pouring, finally relief: My older half brother James returned from a journey to England to establish himself as a Boston printer. I became his apprentice. As an apprentice I toiled twelve hours a day, six days a week, saving more than half of my paltry wages. Serving as an apprentice under the unnecessarily harsh rule of James eventually led me to declare my independence at the age of seventeen, and strike out on my own.

Then to Philadelphia, but only for a single year. Then to England for the promise of something not delivered—a job. And, dear reader, for those who think of the journey from England to America as a brief ten hours, please know that my journey was most often ten long weeks of rolling seas, stale food, clothing stiff with dried sea salt, habitation among a vile-smelling crew, and, if the winds were still and our progress impeded, foul-mooded passengers. Two years I stayed in England, and as a great dry sponge drew in the subtle skills of a master printer and a few, I wished more, attributes of those well-spoken and well-read Londoners.

After two years in England, where I did so enjoy a variety of cultural diversity not visited upon the citizens of my Philadelphia, I returned to America. Once home, a few months as a merchant's clerk, then to work in Keimer's printing shop. But his diligence as to quality was lacking and thereby a source of discomfort to me, as was his offensively dirty and unkempt shop; thus, in 1728, I took my future to my bosom and, as vigorously as a lad in a rowboat pulls for a distant shore in stormy weather, I began my own business, a printing business. Lest you think I oversaw a large enterprise, know that I fetched and transported all supplies, set type, sold advertisements, purchased paper and ink, labored at a press, swept the floor, and composed essays and other writings.

In time, hard time of diligent work, I began to gradually pay off the debt I was under for the printing house. In order to secure my credit and character as a tradesman, I took care not only to be in reality industrious and frugal, but to avoid all appearances to the contrary. I dressed plainly; I was seen at no places of idle diversion; I never went out fishing or shooting. A book, indeed, sometimes debauched me from my work, but that was seldom, and gave no scandal. And to show that I was not above my business, I sometimes brought back to my shop the paper I purchased at the stores through the streets on a wheelbarrow. My efforts to demonstrate diligence of labors were well received and sharply noted by the good citizens of Philadelphia. One merchant wrote:

> The industry of that Franklin is superior to anything I ever saw of the kind. I see him still at work when I go home and he is at work again before his neighbors are out of bed.

At the age of twenty-three I purchased a respected newspaper, the *Pennsylvania Gazette*, from my previous employer, the slovenly Mr. Keimer. The next year, with more than a few pennies saved, I took Deborah Read as my wife. Two years later—as you may recall, "not for the publick good"—I began to write and print *Poor Richard's Almanack*. Thus I became, with good fortune smiling upon me, the author as well as the publisher of the most popular almanack in the Colonies.

With my printing business established, and with my home and wife providing a contented nest, I hoisted a sail into the breeze of public service; first, as clerk to the Pennsylvania Assembly, then as Postmaster. From these public positions, I organized the militia to defend Pennsylvania against the French. With these offices held, and with their attendant responsibilities executed to the fullest, still I was diligent in my labors as a printer, author, publisher, and tradesman; diligent year after year.

In 1748, at the age of forty-two, having begun full-time work at ten years of age, I retired from business. I retired not for leisure. I retired to pursue interests, some in exploration of what were then called the physicals, or, as you would say today, the sciences; others in the realm of public service. Three decades of diligent and steady work, partnered with three decades of frugality and savings, made my choice to retire not a folly.

At forty-two years of age I was known to my fellow citizens of Philadelphia as a rich man—not because I rode in a gilded carriage, or because I beckoned my manservant for whatever menial task was at hand. No, I was known as a rich man because I no longer needed to bring sweat to my brow. Interest from my saved money and fees derived from my well-earned properties delivered sufficient income to provide for my family.

To the point of my essay, then: What is a rich man's fair share of taxes to be paid? If it be no less a percent than any other American, that arrangement would certainly be equitable . . . this is especially so since some would argue that a rich man consumes no more of our government's monies and good offices, perhaps even less, than a poor man; thus, they *should* each pay the same amount of tax dollars. But let me not partake of such an argument. Granted that for a rich man to pay the same percent as all others, that would be fair. Then again, perhaps a greater percent for a rich person would likewise make sense, and certainly not be considered unjust, because even though such persons may have struggled long hours for their riches, luck also shone upon them. Thus, many of the rich would agree, a slightly greater percent for them might do little harm. But!

Do not tax the rich as if levying a punishment upon thieves. Do not tax those who struggled long hours and risked much, as I did, to render them with only an amount remaining after their taxes are paid equal to that of persons who worked less diligently and lived a life of little frugality.

> *Taxes should not be an equalizer of the contentment among the many; taxes must be to the benefit of the many.*
>
> —Poorer Richard's America, *September 2010*

STOPLIGHTS AND WALL STREET

... UNDERSTANDINGS THEREOF

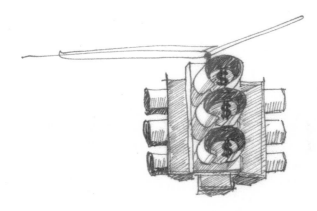

As I advised in my Notes to the Reader, most happenings and occurrences of modern America I understand, while others perplex my logic. Stoplights constitute one such thing that at first I did not comprehend. Why lights of different colors, directing people as a King might direct his subjects from his throne? Would not politeness and courtesy suffice for the efficient intersection and passage of rubber-wheeled conveyances? But in time I came to make sense of it. No need to slow if the light shone green as one approached; no need to stop to see what other traffic might be fast approaching. So easy it seemed once I understood: green to go, red to stop, yellow to speed up.

Wall Street, however, required vastly more effort to comprehend, though at first I thought it an easy task. Several articles I found, several spokesmen I listened to. Thus, in time I came to comprehend the magnificence of Wall Street and its from-on-high commandments, as if chiseled in stone:

- Wall Street firms shall facilitate the purchase of "shares of America" by each and every American.
- Wall Street firms shall buy and sell shares of stock to "make a market," thus assuring an orderly and efficient exchange of shares among shareholders.
- Wall Street firms shall advise and assist American companies in raising capital, thus allowing them to expand and create more wondrous jobs for Americans.

Then more enlightenment: I came to understand even more as I drifted from one office to another in the canyons of Manhattan, listening to Wall Street executives adroitly manage their mighty firms; thus I gleaned insights into other commandments not chiseled in stone, nor recorded anywhere they could be seen:

- Wall Street firms shall ensure that their friends and alumni maintain second homes in the U.S. Treasury and the Federal Reserve.
- Wall Street firms shall seek to maximize profits for their partners in any and all transactions they undertake.
- Wall Street firms shall seek fees from transactions regardless of whether the transaction is good for America, selling subprime-mortgage-backed bonds to teachers' retirement funds; or whether or not the transaction is good for another country, allowing Greece to hide its national deficits by purchasing future revenues of its government.

The second vice is lying, the first is running in debt.

—Poor Richard's, August 1748

- Any Wall Street firm, after losing $10 billion, shall borrow $10 billion from taxpayers; thereupon the firm shall pay its partners $5 billion in bonuses because Wall Street must retain the best and the brightest.

A wolf sheds his coat once a year, his disposition never.

—Poor Richard's, June 1755

HARDSHIPS AND SACRIFICE
... Two Days without Electricity

By far today's Americans little comprehend the sacrifices that their forefathers made; nor do they acknowledge the great extent to which today's Americans benefit from these sacrifices. Be assured, I know that you never made a conscious decision not to pay homage to the past;

you are merely ignorant. Please, do not be offended. I hasten to advise, not ignorance from dullness, but rather an ignorance born of your inability to peer back a score of decades to those generations of Americans who made sacrifices beyond the comprehension of those with heated car seats and convenience stores within a ten-minute drive.

A dim retrospective is not unique to you. Each new generation of Americans can only relate directly to one, two, or perhaps three previous generations. It has always been this way. The second generation of Jamestown colonists more clearly comprehended the harsh sacrifices of the previous generation of starving Virginia colonists than did those of us who signed the Declaration of Independence 150 years later. While not an absolute, in general, each generation of Americans has had it somewhat less challenging than those previous generations. There has been a steady clawing up on the comfort and security curve; thus, each new generation has a less-clear vision or appreciation of the sacrifices and struggles of those first American settlers.

This notion, the notion of not comprehending the hardships of earlier generations of Americans, struck me just recently. I quickly note, dear reader, that my "just recently" is not always calibrated to the same calendar as your "just recently." I was in our Nation's Capital to listen to the president's State of the Union message, one of my many annual pilgrimages. While I will not disclose which president, I will provide two clues to the mystery. The previous year I watched as this same president addressed the Alfalfa Club: an annual calling together in Washington of the nation's powerful to enjoy a fine meal, consume great quantities of Madeira, shovel upon one another criticisms masked as humor, honor the birthday of Confederate general Robert E. Lee, and then consume even more spirits. The president, while standing at a podium addressing a few hundred tuxedo-clad attendees of this celebrated dinner, noted that if Robert E. Lee had been in attendance, the General would have been both 203 years of age and extremely perplexed at the sight of this particular president. Yet another digression. My apologies.

It was a week after this president's first State of the Union address to the nation that Washington, D.C., was covered with a two-foot snowfall, a snowfall of unusual depth for our Capital. Governments were closed. Schools were shuttered. Days before the predicted snowfall, radio and television announcers, in somber voices appropriate for an Ice Age Armageddon, warned all that they might be without electricity for two or three days. Residents were directed to bring in extra stores of food, lest they go hungry; it might take county and state crews days to plow clear village roads. The governors of both Virginia and Maryland, the two states that wrap Washington, D.C., declared a National Emergency, thus assuring a favored place for them at the trough of your Federal Government.

These recent frightful warnings of impending hardship to Washingtonians caused me to reflect on an essay set forth in *Poor Richard's Almanack* of 1748—an essay that recounted the truth of the lives of those settlers in the most northern territories.

The Lakes and standing Waters, which are not above 10 or 12 Feet deep, are frozen to the Ground in Winter, and the Fishes therein all perish. Yet in Rivers near the Sea, and Lakes of a greater depth than 10 or 12 Feet, Fishes are caught all the Winter, by cutting Holes thro' the Ice, and therein putting Lines and Hooks. As soon as the Fish are brought into the open Air, they instantly freeze stiff.

Beef, Pork, Mutton, and Venison, kill'd in the Beginning of the Winter, are preserved by the Frost for Months, entirely free from Putrefecation. Likewise Geese, Partridges, and other Fowls, kill'd at the same Time, and kept with their Feathers on and Guts in, are preserv'd by the Frost, and prove good Eating. All Kinds of Fish are preserv'd in the same Manner.

All the Water they use for Cooking, Brewing, & c. is melted Snow and Ice; no Spring is yet found free from freezing, tho' dug ever so deep down. All Waters inland are frozen fast by the Beginning of Winter, and continue till Spring.

The walls of the Houses are of Stone, two feet thick; the Windows very small, with thick wooden shutters, which are close shut 18 hours every Day in Winter. In the Cellars they put their Wines, Brandies, & c. Large Fires are made every Day, in great Stoves to Warm the Rooms: As soon as the Wood is burnt down to a Coal, the Tops of the Chimnies are close stopped, with an Iron Cover; this keeps the Heat in, but almost stifles the People. And notwithstanding this, in 4 or 5 Hours after the Fire is out, the Inside of the Walls and Bed-places will be 2 or 3 Inches thick with Ice, which is every Morning cut away with a Hatchet. Three or four Times a Day, Iron Shot, of 24 Pounds Weight, are made red hot, and hung up in the Windows of their Apartments, to moderate the Air that comes in at Crevices; yet this, with a Fire kept burning the greatest Part of 24 Hours, will not prevent Beer, Wine, Ink & c. from Freezing.

For their Winter Dress, a Man makes use of three Pair of Socks, of coarse Blanketting, or Duffeld, for the Feet, with a Pair of Deerskin Shoes over them; two Pair of thick English stockings, and a Pair of Cloth Stockings upon them; Breeches lined with Flannel; two or three English Jackets, and a Fur, or Leather Gown over them; a large Beaver Cap, double, to cover over the Face and Shoulders, and a Cloth of Blanketting under the Chin; with Yarn Gloves, and a large Pair of Beaver Mittens, hanging down from the shoulders before, to put the Hands in, reaching up as high as the Elbows. Yet notwithstanding this warm Clothing, those that stir Abroad when any Wind blows from the Northward, are sometimes dreadfully frozen; some have their Hands, Arms, and Face blistered and froze in a terrible manner, the Skin coming off soon after they enter a warm House, and some lose their Toes. And keeping House, or lying-in for the Cure of these Disorders, brings on the Scurvy, which many die of, and few are free from; nothing preventing it but Exercise and stirring Abroad.

Let me return to that recent heavy snowfall in your Nation's Capital: two days with no electricity, three days housebound before workers paid by your government plowed your streets. A National Emergency declared. Ah, the calamity of it all. Faint of heart, I feel.

O Lazy-bones! Dost thou think God would have given thee arms and legs, if he had not design'd thou shoulds't use them.

—Poor Richard's, *December 1739*

GREAT LEADERS LEAD

. . . TODAY'S LEADERS FOLLOW

Leaders must lead. American leaders are elected. To be elected they often perceive they need to follow—follow the polls. So, kind reader, what, you ask, is the problem? If politicians tender overflowing baskets of monies to pollsters so they can mold their campaigns and policies to strike responsive chords with the masses, should you be concerned? The truth of the matter is that democracies are governments administered by those few anointed by the majority. If the tea leaves read by a pollster offer a hopeful candidate, or an insecure incumbent, an insight as to what the majority want, or fear, could not that insight be considered a benefit to the political system?

After much reasoned thought I have come to believe that there are, more likely than not, two nontrivial problems with your polls. One is their sophistication. Today's pollsters slice and dice the voter population into categories and subcategories in an effort to glean insights into diverse clusters and layers of America's population and interest groups. While all these subsets possess common wants and concerns—lower taxes, better education, and less crime—most all subsets have goals unique to them: a tariff on steel imports, a subsidy on cotton, a tax credit for oil exploration, tax relief for church-sponsored schools, release of government property for logging, grants to retrain displaced textile workers, to name only a meager few. Your national political candidate, hoping to maximize his or her harvest of votes, will seek to respond to the greatest number of potential constituent interests possible, only artfully pirouetting around the most controversial and absurd. To ingratiate themselves with the various subsets of voters, incumbent politicians pick up a few large wagonloads of money at the Treasury to fund their constituents' wish lists. This allows the smiling politicians, as you would say, a "photo opportunity" with the newly content farmers, factory workers, oil company executives, and minorities.

Most hurtful for me to say, today's American political system thereby now replicates the Tragedy of Commons put forth by Professor Hardin: If there are not enough fish in the ocean to accommodate all the fishermen, does the collective population of fishermen decide to restrain their harvest of fish, or rather, does each fisherman maximize his catch before there are no more, thus accelerating the decline of the population of our finned food source? As with the fishermen in their trawlers, each subset of Americans wants a fair share of the federal budget, that fair share, dear reader, equaling the maximum any other subgroup is receiving. Do the politicians state there are only so many fish in the sea and dollars in the Treasury? No. They just create more fish. Easily and without a wrinkle of guilt, they borrow more money . . . money to be repaid by those sleeping in your house, and in the other homes of America.

The second problem with pollsters is that they compile an information base, accurate or not, that perversely moves the focus of national leaders from leading to following. Often the national leaders' vision of America's future, as presented to America's citizens, is a carefully crafted mosaic of competing national objectives, thus responding to the diverse multitude of subset population agendas.

In early America there were far fewer agendas competing for national action. America was, from border to border, a nation of farmers, hunters, and fishermen, with a sprinkling of villages and towns, each with their small businesses, perhaps a blacksmith and a dry-goods store, one or two churches, and a schoolhouse. The hopes and fears of a Dover shopkeeper were not dissimilar to those of a shopkeeper in Concord. Concerns of a farmer in Harrisburg were the same as those of a farmer in Williamsburg. Neither the American population, nor American commerce, was diverse. The national political platform could thus be precise and concise. Not so today. To be effective, today's leaders must exercise triage; they must choose the most important goals for a Nation and then push its citizens to achieve those goals. And until those goals are achieved, strong leaders may not permit themselves to be swayed from the most important by the loud cries of those that are less so.

Bargaining has neither friends nor relations.
—Poor Richard's, *April 1736*

And while leaders must limit the goals of a nation, a leader must also be prepared to lead in a direction others believe ill-advised. In the history of America, when a bold leader set the direction for the nation, often that course was not the easiest for the country, nor was it a course that most citizens might have chosen . . . at that moment. "Let's pay them their Stamp Tax; after all, they built the ships that got us here." "A house divided can stand; just make those people live in the barn." "The only thing we have to fear is fear itself, but things will work themselves out; just be patient." "It's Europe's war; if England falls, it falls." The above revised classical quotes prove that the easiest course for America was not always taken. Nor was the course taken always the wish of most Americans, at the moment. But history has proven that the correct course *was* taken—even if the American leaders who made those tough decisions were not always popular at the time.

With an elegance that I haven't heard since "Before the end of the decade, we will send a man to the moon and return him safely," past American leaders pleaded their justifications as to why Americans needed to sacrifice for a worthy cause. Then they took resolute action. They did not worship the pollster god.

Your leaders are not leading; rather, they equivocate and attempt to respond to all, and in doing such, they follow, thus exercising a natural attribute of the American personality: Mend all wrongs, cause no pain. But as a general must husband his resources and see men die so that the battle is won, no less responsibility and heartache must a national leader endure in the wars against nation-ending policies.

To serve the Publick faithfully, and at the same time please it entirely, is impractical.
—Poor Richard's, *October 1758*

INFORMATION CARESSED IS KNOWLEDGE

... INFORMATION CHURNED IS CLUTTER

Other than father to son, or teacher to student, most information of my day, knowledge of my day, was conveyed by books—books that were coveted by those without, guarded by those with. Most fortunate was I when a book was lent to me; I would savor it as a sweet custard ...

a custard slowly eaten. In time, with a small sum laboriously saved, I purchased my first book: a much-used copy of John Bunyan's *The Pilgrim's Progress*. After reading and rereading till its thoughts and messages were imprinted on my mind, as dried ink on paper, this book was sold and another purchased.

In time, no need was there for me to sell one cherished book to purchase another; rather, a modest library in my home was sufficient: a library of great thoughts, a library of inflexible principles, and a library of the human character. And, I am proud to say, I helped to incorporate the Library Company of Philadelphia in the year 1731; thus, the average citizen could quench his thirst for knowledge.

You, dear citizens, possess in one small electronic device perched on your desk, or nested in your waistcoat pocket, all the information of my world, and of your world. You may ask this device what day of the week was July 4, 1776, demand that it list Aristotle's teachings, advise you as to the average rainfall in Guam in April, print for you the poignant words of Dr. Martin Luther King's last speech, or immediately calculate 42.142616 to the second power.

But, as I peer over your shoulders, I do not observe you savoring the information and knowledge gleaned from these devices; I do not see you caressing newly learned facts. Most often, your wondrous electronic machines are tasked with the mundane and the nonsensical. They transmit your random, wandering thoughts to others. In turn, they message you with the most trivial. At day's end, many of you proudfully boast of hundreds of messages received, hundreds sent. To what end? Any knowledge gained to guide you in your life's journey? Any truths gleaned of the human spirit? More likely, "Just took a shower, great new shampoo, call you later."

And, another observation. Other than conversation of person-to-person or person-to-persons, communication of my day was as a stalk of corn growing. If, when sitting by a window in my Craven Street, London, townhouse (I let rooms from Margaret Stevenson), I wrote a letter to my friend and ally in dealing with the Penns of Pennsylvania, Mr. Joseph Galloway in America, it would be at best *five months* till I received a letter in response. If the weather was not favorable, seven months might be necessary.

You, friends, are minutes from message sent and response received. Amazing, wonderful . . . but! Many of life's events are best played as a game of chess, not hand-ball. Too many Americans think that how quickly they answer a question is the mark of intelligence. No, kind ladies and gentlemen: The mark of intelligence is how well the answer is crafted—crafted to obtain the most and offend the least.

And, please know: A message charged with emotion that is quickly sent allows no opportunity to reconsider once the emotion has evaporated (recall my strong letter to Mr. Stratham of the House of Commons, a letter never posted).

FEDERAL INCOME TAXES

... Should We Reconsider the Stamp Act?

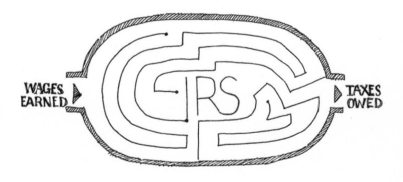

To replenish its Treasury after a long war with France, on February 13, 1765, the British House of Commons passed the Stamp Act. This Act required American colonists to purchase government-issued stamps from England; the appropriate number of stamps had to be affixed to each and every legal document, newspaper, pamphlet, almanack, and advertisement exchanged in the Colonies. My Pennsylvania and the other Colonies of America saw no advantage for them in this newly mandated tax, thus they resisted; they challenged England's right to levy a tax on normal commerce. One year later, I appeared before members of the British Parliament to argue the arbitrary nature of the Stamp Act; responding to a question put to me about this tax, I spoke the unsugared words, "It is intended to extort our money from us, or ruin us by the consequences of refusing to pay it."

Three weeks after my appearance before Parliament, the House of Commons passed a motion to repeal the Stamp Act, and King George III assented. Thus, in 1766, the Stamp Tax that had been laid upon America was swept away.

Leap forward with me now 147 years from the repeal of the Stamp Act; refer to the Sixteenth Amendment, ratified on February 3, 1913, to the U.S. Constitution. This amendment gave birth to the right of the Federal Government to tax the incomes of each and every American citizen. As with almost all constitutional amendments, it was of a few words; only thirty, to be precise:

> The Congress shall have the power to lay and collect taxes on incomes, from whatever source derived, without apportionment among the several States, and without requiring any census or enumeration.

As an acorn grows to a mighty oak, these thirty acorns grew and multiplied to a dense forest with a thick ground cover of bramble bushes and poison ivy.

The Office of the Chief Counsel of the Internal Revenue Service recently reported that today's Tax Code, which codifies the thirty-word Sixteenth Amendment, has grown to 3.7 million words . . . recall, the nearest star was 4.5 million light-years from our sun. Since 3.7 million words in and of itself is of little meaning to most Americans, allow me to calibrate an order of magnitude. For those believers among you, 3.7 million words is equal to the word count of five Bibles, forty-nine Korans, or forty-three Torahs. For you nonbelievers, 3.7 million words equates to 220 copies of *Cosmopolitan* or 195 copies of *Playboy* . . . as a curious retired printer, I peruse most all publications.

Alas, the 3.7 million words of the Tax Code are devoid of an engaging plot or any interesting emotional play among diverse characters. Our nation's Tax Code is a labyrinth of twisted, complex sentences that intertwine and bind in utter confusion even the most diligent taxpayer. A sample—no alterations made—from the instruction for a single line, Line 3, of Form 8801: Credit for Minimum Tax is as follows:

> *Your Minimum Tax Credit Net Operating Loss Deduction is the excess of the deductions (excluding the Minimum Tax Credit Net Operating Loss Deduction) over the income used to figure Alternative Minimum Taxable Income taking into account only exclusion items. Figure this excess with the modifications in section 172(d) taking into account only exclusion items. (That is, the section 172(d) modifications must be figured separately for the Minimum Tax Credit Net Operating Loss Deduction.) For example, the limitation of nonbusiness deductions to the amount of nonbusiness income must be figured sepa-*

rately for the Minimum Tax Credit Net Operating Loss Deduction using only nonbusiness income and deductions but taking into account only exclusion items. However, ignore the disallowance of the deduction for personal exemptions under section 172(d)(3), because it has already been taken into account to figure Alternative Minimum Taxable Income attributable only to exclusion items.

If tax-compliance businesses and services were to be classified as an industry, that industry would be one of the largest in the United States. To perform the estimated 7.6 billion hours of tax preparation and review work, the "tax industry" requires the equivalent of 3.8 million full-time workers. By way of painful comparison, that is twice as many people as constituted the entire population of the Colonies when the Stamp Act was levied upon us by England.

The complexity—a euphemism for absurdity—of the Tax Code spawns perverse outcomes. Patriotic taxpayers who seek to comply with the law often make inadvertent errors, causing them to either overpay their tax or become subject to IRS enforcement actions for mistaken underpayment of tax. Meanwhile, the gentle and sophisticated American (that is to say, rich) taxpayers often employ professionals to find esoteric Tax Code provisions that enable them to legitimately reduce their tax liabilities.

The reason for both the complexity and staggering size of the Tax Code is the avalanche of "one-off" type of tax provisions—provisions that provide unique tax benefits to a select (lucky) few. Let us consider Hedge Fund Managers, folks who manage the monies of others. In 2009, scores of them received compensation of more than $1 billion each;

yes, that's not a misprint: $1 billion or more for each set of two ears. The highest individual compensation was $4 billion for the year, this annual sum being equal to $330 million a month, $10 million a day, or $400,000 per hour . . . twenty-four hours each and every day. Let me doff my hat for a moment to all these successful Hedge Fund Managers . . . but . . .

In a previous essay I set forth my belief that most of America's rich pay their fair share of taxes. Note well, I suggested *most*, not *all*. Logic would demand that the difference between most and all is some; hence, some do not pay their fair share.

Let's consider tax rates for a few brief moments. America has a progressive tax rate: The more dollars earned, the higher the tax rate. However, individual Americans are taxed differently for two types of income: ordinary income, salaries, tips, et cetera; and capital gains, property sold for a gain. The tax rate for ordinary income rises to 35 percent. Capital gains tax rates do not exceed 15 percent. The low rate for capital gains is, in part, justified by not wanting to tax Americans on inflation. A house is purchased for $50,000 in 1980, and sold for $100,000 in 2000; capital gains of 15 percent is paid on the $50,000 gain.

So what tax rate do the Hedge Fund Managers pay who made billions of dollars a year? The lowest rate—15 percent, the capital gains rate. Thus, one would assume the well-paid Fund Manager must have purchased property (assets) that appreciated. No; he managed assets that appreciated, and his fee was a percent of the increase. He risked nothing. He owned no assets or property. Hence, he could not have owned properties that appreciated.

Why do Hedge Fund Managers pay a lower rate than other professionals? More important, why do they pay a far lower rate than many of the teachers, shopkeepers, nurses, and ministers in their communities who make less in a year than they make in half an hour? Read carefully my essay on the Branches of Government. But below, a preview.

Hedge Fund Managers employed excellent lobbyists to represent them in Washington in 2007, and they pulled a few tens of millions of dollars from their waistcoat pockets to tender campaign contributions that same year. Why 2007? Could it be that was the year when the tax rate applicable to Hedge Fund Managers was debated in Congress?

Ah! Yes, it certainly was.

18

CEASING TO LIVE VERSUS DYING

. . . DON'T SEVER MY HEAD TO SAVE ME

For several long months my Market Street home was the village of my life. Bodily strength had taken its leave in anticipation that my soul was soon to depart. But my intellect, in whatever meager portion the Supreme Being bestowed upon me, continued to reside comfortably between my ears.

During the last few weeks, as the good Earth's winter turned to spring in that year of 1790, while my life's fall turned to a final winter, much pleasure I took in rereading past letters and essays and, as strength permitted, drafting missives to old correspondents, the last to my most respected friend, Thomas Jefferson. Seldom were there days not interrupted with kind acquaintances and public servants seeking, more for politeness' sake than a felt need, my advice on matters of little weight. And most welcome were those few gentlemen with the hours to spare, and a temperament to lose, who played cribbage with me from one meal to the next.

In nature's time the tide of my life receded; no crashing waves of new experiences rolled in; only calm tidal pools of life's remembrances remained. For these remembrances I was grateful, having raised myself from humble beginnings to, by the application of studious effort, a rank among men that I could not imagine again, in any other lifetime, achieving. In my home, in my bed, with my most loving daughter Sally kneeling beside me, with my grandson Benny holding my hand, with my cherished memories within me, I closed my eyes with a warm blanket of peace wrapping my body, and my soul.

Why, tearful reader, do I relate the events of my last days? As a contrast; to either compare or contrast, there must be two or more occurrences, objects, or theories. As a contrast with my death, let me discuss a letter written by my Scottish friend of many decades, Sir John Pringle. He was a physician who had been on several occasions a most pleasurable traveling companion to me. Perhaps we were friends because both of us held a wide and deep curiosity about nature and the physicals of our world.

I had written from Passy, as you may recall, a village not a far distance from Paris; I wrote of toads that were found alive at a quarry, even though they had been entombed in a rock cavity with no air or substance. In Sir Pringle's letter recounting an event not unlike the entombed frogs, my good physician friend set forth the particulars of his experiments with large moths; Mosquito Hawks, they were called. If one such moth, after being restrained, was put under a glass bowl and shielded from light, it would live a mere few days. But if, Sir Pringle recounted, the head of the moth was carefully removed by the tiniest and most sharp of knives, and then the moth was put under a glass hidden from light, with small movement of legs and wings showing such, it would live for as long as eighty days.

Fellow citizens, easily I passed from life to the beyond while lying in my bed, in my home of many years, among those who loved me. You, dear friends, when life's far horizon draws so near, allow your most highly trained and skilled physicians to place you in a hospital of no friends, of no family, of no remembrances. Once there, these physicians remove your head, thus delaying your death, but not extending your life in any manner desirable.

God heals, and the doctor takes the fee.
—Poor Richard's, November 1736

I hasten to advise that the essay just laid before you was not written to scorn hospitals. Know that in concert with the good doctor, Thomas Bond, I secured sufficient subscriptions to fund, and thus build, Philadelphia's first hospital, opened in the fall of 1755—a hospital to tend to the healing, not to the dying, of my fellow citizens.

THE WRITTEN WORD
. . . YESTERDAY'S PRINTING, TODAY'S MEDIA

H ere is a favorite excerpt of mine from *Poor Richard's Almanack* of 1750:

> *What an admirable invention is writing, by which a man may communicate his mind without opening his*

mouth, and at 1,000 leagues distance, and even to future ages, only by the help of 22 letters, which may be joined 5,852,616,738,497,664,000 ways, and will express all things in a very narrow compass. 'Tis a pity this excellent act has not preserved the name and memory of its inventor.

While the written word is surely a wonderful gift, it does permit, as does the executioner's black hood, the deliverer of a message to remain unseen. And I came to understand that anonymous slander is most harshly delivered; a hood of anonymity emboldens the writer, thus, in turn, stoking the reader's anger.

> *There's small revenge in words, but words may be greatly revenged.*
> —Poor Richard's, August *1735*

At all times as a publisher of the *Pennsylvania Gazette*, I deleted those items that were malicious, and not verifiable by facts. Whenever I was solicited to insert anything of mean-spirited slander, and the writers pleaded the liberty of the press—saying that a newspaper was like a stagecoach, in which anyone who paid had the right to a place—my answer was that I would print the piece separately, and the author might have as many copies as he so pleased to distribute himself, but I would not spread his detrition. Having contracted with my subscribers of Philadelphia to furnish them with what might be useful, I could not fill their papers with anything otherwise.

Written, printed, and spoken words were the only, as you would say, media available in my world. The American media of today is instantaneous, inescapable, and all-surrounding. Obviously, then, there is no less need, and perhaps greater need, to avoid slander . . . or any shadings of facts to render an event, organization, or person other than how it actually is.

Alas, as I watch your news, news reported over the airwaves to tens of millions of citizens' ears, I fear the legs of fair reporting do not always straddle an issue; at times they seem to kick it to one side or another. And, many of those that report the news appear to commingle their opinion with the flow of facts, thus relieving the listener of the need to draw his own conclusions. If, perchance, some of America's news personalities became judges, they might well sentence the accused before the jury rendered its verdict.

Each human right holds a firm hand with its partner, human responsibility. The Bill of Rights ensured Freedom of Speech. Who holds that hand?

AN IGNORANT MAN WITH NO EDUCATION IS TO BE PITIED

... AN IGNORANT MAN WITH AN EDUCATION IS TO BE FEARED

On a bright summer day in 1753, I received, with much unnecessary ceremony, an honorary Master of Arts Degree from Yale College, presented that day to me by the Reverend Thomas Clap. More than two centuries later I watched your President John F. Kennedy, a

Harvard graduate, accept an honorary degree from Yale. That summer afternoon, while addressing the university's graduating class of 1962, and with his toothy grin hinting at the emotion to follow, President Kennedy declared, "It might be said now that I have the best of both worlds, a Yale degree and a Harvard education." I too had the best of both worlds in 1753: a freshly printed degree from Yale and a superb education, not from Harvard, but rather an education drawn from years well spent as a tradesman, a merchant, a public servant, and a citizen of Philadelphia, where I worked, spoke, debated, ate, drank, and sang with other citizens of that great city. Citizens who, as you would now say, "all worked for a living."

Thus, my education was that of common sense gained from embracing the common man. Sorry, I am, that common sense is neither a subject nor a science any college has dared to codify, or otherwise lay to paper, so that it could be taught and the appropriate degree awarded. Rather, common sense is both a collection of insights, gleaned from life experiences, that show the truth of human strengths and frailties, and, of no less importance, an understanding of those most primary realities of commerce and nature that mark the paths men follow . . . for good or for grief.

He was so learned that he could name a horse in nine languages. So ignorant that he bought a cow to ride on.

—Poor Richard's, *November 1750*

As with many differences of life and man, those differences in learning and education serve well as matches to ignite the fires of prejudice. To the uneducated, the gentleman of letters is a man of soft hands, no worldly skills, a condescending manner, and an air of entitlement and intellectual superiority. To the educated person, the common man—the farmer, the laborer, the skilled tradesman—earns his keep by physical effort and holds little intellectual curiosity; thus, he only considers the most simple issues of life.

The uneducated man may be smarter than most believe. The educated man is often less smart than most believe.
—Poorer Richard's America, *September 2010*

A desirable human intellect would possess both a common sense acquired and nurtured through the everyday commerce of a working man, blended with a formal education steeped in the arts, letters, and the physicals. But the most desirable intellect would be possessed of all that above and crowned with a fine gray cap of wisdom. Wisdom is that attribute of man that only appears to those who have lived sufficient days to experience life's challenges, and, having done such, pondered the import of these challenges, both good and poor; and then, prudently aware of their triumphs and mistakes in meeting such challenges, those blessed with wisdom adjust their life's perspectives, expectations, and actions.

It would seem, I suggest for your consideration, that within today's Federal Government, there is a bias for embracing the well-educated. This bias would do no harm if its partner was a bias toward the well-experienced wearing a cap of wisdom. I fear that too many government officials, both elected and appointed, are placed in positions of grading eggs without ever having seen a chicken or having cracked a shell over a skillet.

The learned fool writes his nonsense in better language than the unlearned; but still 'tis nonsense.
— Poor Richard's, July 1754

Ponder this: America's appointed National Economic Council consists of persons who have written tome-like books on economics and finance, lectured at the most prestigious schools, and served on bank boards and Federal Reserve Boards. But alas, not one has taken out a second mortgage to pay his employees. None has pleaded with a bank to extend the line of credit that finances needed farm equipment; none has suffered the IRS threatening to lock his doors because he was a few days late with a quarterly FICA payment; and none has had OSHA coldly advise him that he was being fined $5,000 because his ladder—yes, one ladder—failed to meet code. Alternatively stated: The persons of the National Economic Council do not use Hamburger Helper or, as we would have said, "eat the tail of the pig."

A book on how to best court a maiden should not be written by one who has yet to kiss a lass.
                    —Poorer Richard's America, *September 2010*

While those educated Americans with position often, with their plumage of pompous and ill-advised actions, render themselves colorful targets for those hardworking Real Americans—a term defined by self-proclaimed hardworking Real Americans—many well-educated Americans with position are truly worthy of respect and admiration. They are not elitist. And while America's first great explorers succeeded because of strength of character and of back (Lewis and Clark's exploration of American Western lands during my friend Thomas Jefferson's administration), the exploration of space relies upon strength of character and intellect: astronauts with PhDs supported by thousands of NASA engineers and scientists.

The future of America is not ignorance.
                    —Poorer Richard's America, *September 2010*

For our dear America, the most important is not which citizens are the most important: the well-educated or the well-worked. The most important is that for America to prosper, *all* Americans must acknowledge that both the well-educated and the well-worked citizens are worthy of the respect of the other. Such respect demands that neither group accuse the other of being either highbrow, insensitive, liberal elitists or ignorant, rifle-hugging, pick-up-driving crazies.

> *Joe Six-Pack and Two-Martinis Mike make a potent pair.*
> —Poorer Richard's America, *September 2010*

MARITAL BLISS

. . . Till Discovered

No different. More than two centuries and no difference, the young lass and the gentleman of wisdom . . . wisdom being a kindness of word choice, *age* the better word, age being the toll for wisdom; but perhaps certainly not wisdom. If wisdom were present, why would one dangle his organ of delight near a sausage grinder . . . where was I going with these thoughts? More simply stated, men and women of my century smiled, flirted, and beyond. And as with America of today, marriage was not always a well-built fence containing lust and intrigue.

A difference, though; a difference between my days on Earth and yours today. A veil descended in my day to protect the innocent and to sequester the guilty in their private shame. Not so today; once caught, once disclosed as an unfaithful husband in the public domain, for reasons not understood by me—perhaps some need for self-mutilation or moral public nudity—the humbled and shameful husband of today stands before your media and confesses his sins.

The end of passion is the beginning of repentance.
—Poor Richard's, *February 1749*

But the husband's public confession is not the most mystifying of this modern spectacle to me. Slightly behind and to one side stands the wife, a wife rigid in a stunned bewilderment wrapping her embarrassed mortification. Should not the lass, rather than the wife, share the shame of the husband? Let the young woman of the immoral tryst stand behind the repentant, humbled husband. Better the emotionally wounded wife spend her time in the loving embrace of family, friends, and attorneys.

And there's a lust in man no charm can tame,
Of loudly publishing our neighbor's shame;
On eagles' wings immortal scandals fly,
While virtuous actions are but borne to die.

—Juvenal

And yes, I know, curious reader. Yes, I know that some have written of my "eagle's wings"; they have written of those years from 1776 till 1785, when I resided in France. During the first of these years I was most busy negotiating an alliance with France—loans and safe ports for America's ships—and then in the latter years, I shepherded through, with John Jay and John Adams, the Treaty of Paris with Great Britain that marked our peace with her at the end of our hard-fought Revolutionary War.

It is certainly true that many women friends and, perhaps, admirers were in my company those nine years. But I was not a lecherous, balding pretender of romance. Even if my mind wished to be lecherous, my worn body of over seventy years had long before abdicated its right to join in any romantic campaign of physical conquest. Rather, if I seduced, it was a seduction of the mademoiselle's intellect and femininity, this done by the application of large portions of my attention, my charm, and, as I could muster, my American Revolutionary mystique. I had then, as you might say, many soul mates of the opposite gender. Soul mates, no more.

And, kind sirs and ladies, if you dismiss my pleading of French chastity, please recall that I was a widower.

Deborah, my Debby, my most attentive wife of forty-four years, had departed my world two years before I first represented America's interests, which were then only hopes, in that faraway France of my imagined notoriety.

UNINTENDED CONSEQUENCES, DOMESTIC AFFAIRS

... DAD, MOM, AND THE TWO KIDS OWE AN EXTRA $10,600

As you sadly know so well, your America had to quickly reach deep into its pocket in 2008 to beat back a financial calamity of a magnitude frightening to ponder. You were within a few days of ATMs calling a work stoppage. The worst of it is that America did not reach into its pocket to retrieve money; it pulled out a well-used pen and used it once again to scrawl America's signature to IOUs . . . IOUs totaling $700 billion. On bended knees America tendered many of these IOUs, in the form of U.S. Treasury bonds, to China in exchange for their cash. Cash saved from profits derived from hundreds of millions of energetic Chinese laborers sweating long hours to produce goods purchased by smiling Americans flashing their well-worn credit cards . . . a topic for an essay to follow.

A single industry was the benefactor of the newly issued IOUs: wayward American banks. Such institutions received the $700 billion via the Troubled Asset Repurchase Program (TARP). More aptly, this program should have been labeled the Flimsy Asset Repurchase Tax . . . you may compile the initials and construct the acronym.

Many theories and indictments were put forth by indignant legislators and scores of newly anointed financial sages to explain why our banks, long thought to be granite blocks of America's financial foundation, were on the public dole: incompetent management, greedy executives, Wall Street manipulation, real estate speculators, unrepentant consumerism . . . a selection of the accused. One theory not put forth by any elected official was that of the unintended dire consequences of America's benevolent intentions. By your leave, permit me to meander on.

For more than a hundred years local banks helped local citizens to buy homes by providing long-term loans. Before making a home loan—a mortgage, as it was called—the banker, that man entrusted to safeguard the deposits of townspeople, looked the borrower in the eye. Likely the banker may have known him for years; he may have known his parents as well. The banker likely knew the man who employed the seeker of the loan and the builder who built the house he sought to purchase. The hoped-for mortgage was only made for a portion of the cost of the home; the borrower had to demonstrate fiscal responsibility (offering proof that he could earn and save) by having enough cash in his possession to make a significant down payment.

Fannie Mae and Freddie Mac were created by Congress, as two government-sponsored enterprises, to guarantee mortgages made by thousands of local American banks in hundreds of localities. These Fannie and Freddie loans were guaranteed by those American taxpayers you see in your family picture on the mantel. As with the first half of the *Titanic*'s ocean voyage, Fannie Mae and Freddie Mac enjoyed tranquil sailing as they enforced traditional lending criteria on all those local banks issuing loans that they in turn guaranteed. Then the iceberg loomed ahead, in the familiar American guise of good intentions.

At the turn of the century, the most recent century, Affordable Housing Goals were established by the Federal Government. They required Fannie and Freddie to purchase from banks $2.4 trillion—no, fearful reader, it is trillion, not billion—of mortgages that taxpayers would guarantee. The smiling faces in the family photograph would soon seem less so. To help low-income individuals buy their first homes, banks no longer needed to look a borrower in the eye to make certain that repayment was likely. Rather, no down payments were required, no meaningful proof of income was demanded, and often the initial interest rates charged were below true market rates.

Simply stated, with the government lowering the standards under which mortgages were made, and, by purchasing all the mortgages a bank could process and fund, the Country enjoyed a Mardi Gras marathon of building, buying, and speculating. And it was to the economic benefit of every bank and mortgage broker to place as many loans as possible. Process a loan, collect a fee, then sell the loan to Fannie and Freddie. No need to be bothered as to whether the purchaser could afford the house payments once Fannie and Freddie bought it.

Pray don't burn my house to roast your eggs.
—Poor Richard's, *January 1751*

As buzzards flock to a rotting deer, Wall Street's denizens soon appeared. Sensing the mortgage flow possessed a wondrously wide and deep canal of funds, they eagerly created the most eloquent financial derivatives, thus permitting them to cast their nets into the swift-flowing financial waters and pull out great catches of profits. Hundreds of millions of dollars of fees were swiftly harvested from selling Triple-A-rated mortgage-backed bonds. The Triple-A rating related only to the polished marble facade of the bond, not to its pig-slop core. Many of these bonds were eagerly purchased by fiscally fragile municipalities that, in a painfully short time, came to understand, as the bonds defaulted, that the Triple-A rating possessed the same financial reality as the Tooth Fairy.

Bless their hearts, compassionate legislators and government officials had tried to help those with meager wages to purchase homes. A righteous and well-intended cause, doubtless, no? However: "Might doesn't make right"; neither does "Right make might." Merely because America attempts to do the right thing, the outcome may well not be best for America; in fact, it may not be survivable for America. Kindhearted plans, noble intentions—they can all go astray if not well administered and monitored. Scores of institutions and armies of peoples are watching and waiting for America to take actions, benevolent or not, that may be exploited for their own benefit, not for America's.

And, dear taxpayer, there are reasons, sound reasons, that over the centuries protocols, regulations, and rules of thumb have been recognized and refined to assure the integrity of financial institutions. Avoiding them, or discarding them, for no other purpose than to exercise benevolence for a portion of Americans can well jeopardize all Americans, and America itself.

America must only exercise its benevolence from a position of strength.

Great good-nature, without prudence, is a great misfortune.

—*Author unknown*

23

YOU HAVE A PROBLEM

. . . WELCOME TO PLANET EARTH

Unpleasant and hurtful occurrences visit us all. The most arbitrary episodes of grief will, at times, assail and overwhelm even those with a stout heart and disposition. Often something adverse occurs for no rational reason . . . lightning strikes. Perhaps, though, there is a reason: the actions or inactions of an individual; standing in the center of a soybean field during a frighteningly powerful gray-black thunderstorm.

Many of you, my fellow citizens, have cultivated a propensity to blame others for your hurts, often by instituting a lawsuit over an unfortunate circumstance, or by soliciting your government to render an unhappiness less so. Before doing either, make a most honest appraisal of your culpability. Alas, be warned: Often the effort—a legal action—to correct a perceived wrong and collect restitution consumes monies and emotional energies far beyond any potential awards. Our American legal system is not a lottery; some small slight should not be the opportunity to seek the pot at the end of a rainbow.

> *Neglect kills injuries, revenge increases them.*
> —Poor Richard's, *October 1749*

In fairness and equity, I must confess the truth of this matter. As the following excerpt from *Poor Richard's Almanack* of 1744 does confess, my generation also enjoyed a propensity to seek legal redress.

> *Two traveling Beggars, (I've forgot their Name)*
> *An Oyster they found to which they both laid Claim.*
> *Warm the Dispute! At length to Law they'd go,*
> *As richer Fools for Trifles often do.*
> *The Cause two Petty-foggers undertake,*
> *Resolving right or wrong some Gain to make.*
> *They jangle till the Court this Judgment gave,*

Determining what every one should have.
The friendly Law's impartial Care:
Half Shell for him, Half Shell for thee;
Oyster's meat the Bench and Lawyer's Fee.

BILL OF RIGHTS
. . . FLAG BURNING AND ARMOR-PIERCING AMMO

Of all the discussions and debates that I eavesdrop upon—and since no one knows that I am listening, it must, by any reasonable application of logic, be considered eavesdropping—of all conversations, the most fascinating are those wherein eminent scholars, and less-eminent politicians, expound upon the true intentions of the Founding Fathers. Often, to my smiling amazement, such discourse offers the most insightful nuances of our thinking during that summer of 1789 when, after much debate, the Bill of Rights was incorporated into our nation's newborn Constitution. And within the Bill of Rights, it is the First and the Second Amendments that are most confidently, and at times emotionally, interpreted by scholars whose great-great-grandfathers were born more than a century after the Bill of Rights was ratified.

> I *shook the hand of a man who shook the hand of a person of position, thus I know well a person of position.*
>
> —Poorer Richard's America, *September 2010*

Before I wade into a dark pool of snakes, permit me to set before you a brief primer on a most narrow portion of law: the Rule of the Absurd. This rule dictates that if there are two ways to interpret a term in a contract, or in another document or regulation, and one interpretation is absurd, then the other interpretation, the non-absurd one, is utilized. For example, a newly married young man purchases a $1,000 life insurance policy and a $500 disability policy. The latter pays if, by misfortune of an accident, he is unable to work. An unfortunate lad indeed he is, for a fortnight after purchasing the two policies he is killed in an accident. In time, a dutiful insurance agent tenders a $1,000 payment to the young lad's tearful wife, who then asks, where might be the $500, since her husband was also totally disabled by his death and, hence, was rendered unable to work.

While our deceased young man was, in truth, unable to work while lying quite still in his pine coffin, the court would rule it was absurd, when considered rationally in the context of one policy being for death and one for disability, to collect on both insurance policies. The court would have applied common sense, a notion not in attendance lately when the Bill of Rights is, like a man being drawn and quartered, stretched to absurd interpretations by many of today's sages of Constitutional Law. I humbly submit to you, but not without a belief in the righteousness of what I submit, that your courts at times have not utilized the notion of the Rule of the Absurd, but rather rendered absurd rulings when considering the intents of the First and Second Amendments.

> *There is no surer way to misread any document than to read it literally.*
>
> —Billings Learned Hand

Normally, in my life's tasks, I undertook the most difficult as my first. Let me build my courage for the Second Amendment. Let me initially discuss the less emotionally raw First Amendment.

As background for my discussion, please take to your heart the cause and purpose of the Bill of Rights. These rights were drafted to assuage those Founding Fathers who warned that the Constitution of the United States, in all its written glory, failed to protect the basic principles of human liberty. Please, for emphasis, let me repeat: They exist to ensure human liberty. To provide a robust and unambiguous statement as to those rights of the citizens of the United States, the Bill of Rights was, as a series of amendments to the Constitution, attached to, and made part of that wondrous document. Among other rights, the First Amendment provided for "freedom of speech."

As we consider the First Amendment, let us ask ourselves, if perchance we would have had the occasion to visit President Washington in 1789, the year the Bill of Rights was introduced by James Madison, this President Washington who as Commanding General of the Continental Army saw his men fight and die for America; a General whose very soul was torn apart during the long Valley Forge winter, where his men with their frozen feet wrapped in rags, wearing gaunt faces of despair, did not desert him for the warmth of family and home; a General who knew that if the war for independence was lost, he and America's Founding Fathers would likely be hanged as traitors—ask this General, as President of the United States, if the right of freedom of speech allowed for the burning of a flag that, with its stripes and stars together, is no less than a monument of our nation waving in the free winds of America.

No, I think not. I know not. President Washington would, with all his energies and passion, argue, with a conviction fueled by rage, that flag burning was most certainly not a protected right.

If you do not embrace my argument, if you discard it as patriotic emotionalism, let me propose another. Noah Webster, a lexicographer of fame and stature, was a man I knew and much admired. In the latest dictionary and thesaurus printed under his banner, I noted that the following synonymous adjectives are offered as qualities to describe a noun I will disclose in a moment: *coarse, nasty, obscene,* and *vulgar.* These synonymous adjectives, I would humbly submit, could be descriptors of flag burning. But it is not flag burning that is referred to; Webster provides the synonyms to characterize a term not protected by the First Amendment: *pornography.*

So, dear and confused reader, permit me to stir the boiling pot more vigorously. If President Washington and the other Founding Fathers were shown a painting of an American burning the Stars and Stripes, and another painting of two nude young lasses and a blacksmith frolicking in the hay, an act your courts might call pornography, which painting might the Founding Fathers agree was protected under the First Amendment?[2] Neither, dear reader. Neither would be considered to be protected by the First Amendment as an instance of Freedom of Speech. And if you were to ask which painting was the more egregious and more worthy of *not* being defended under the First Amendment, the unanimous answer from them would be: the burning of the American flag. No rightful extrapolation of the intentions of the drafters of the Bill of Rights encompasses the desecration of the American flag.

And even if misinterpreting the intentions of our nation's founders is removed from this essay, your laws

---

[2] Knowing the Founding Fathers as I did, having spent many delightful evenings with them at a diverse sampling of taverns, a few would certainly wish to study the paintings intently before rendering a well-crafted opinion.

are not consistent, not consistent in protecting our flag. If, as a citizen of today's America, you were to spit on a single congressman's face, you could well be charged with an offense. If you were to spit on the pavement where he stood, or anyone else stood, you might still be charged. But if you were to spit on our country's face, our flag, within its closely woven threads the wisps of those souls of a million men who have died for our country, why would that, to spit on our flag, not be the most grievous offense? No, we did not intend, we did not allow, that you could desecrate our flag.

> *Oh, say does that star-spangled banner yet wave*
> *O'er the land of the free and the home of the*
> *brave?*
>
> —Francis Scott Key, 1814

I brace myself for the paragraphs to follow that speak to the Second Amendment, which in all its less-than-perfect grammar and quizzical structure declares:

> *A well-regulated Militia, being necessary to the secu-*
> *rity of a free State, the right of the People to keep and bear*
> *Arms, shall not be infringed.*

Think back with me to the 1770s and 1780s. America had no armies of substance. My America won the Revo-lutionary War with farmers, hunters, fishermen, shop-keepers, and other ordinary citizens fighting as one army; many of these citizen soldiers fought with their own weapons. Weapons that before the war were not weapons, but rather their hunting muskets.

If, at the time of the discussion of the Second Amendment by the First Congress, a bright light from above had washed over the chamber and a deep voice from a location not known boomed out, "America, in time, will have armies and navies greater than all the other nations of the world together; thus, there is no need for a militia," those present who did not faint dead away from the grave theatrics of the moment would have thought this worldly prediction never could come to be. Even if, for whatever reasons imagined, the prediction from a voice on high had been accepted as all-knowing, every member of the chamber would have been, I am confident in declaring, most pleased to have the Second Amendment merely state

The People shall have the right to keep and bear Arms.

Muskets were an everyday part of American life when the Bill of Rights was drafted. As you would say, we did not have to hang our hat on the need for a militia to allow Americans to bear arms. If an American desired to hunt or to guard his home with a musket, so be it. But as with the First Amendment, the Second has been drawn and quartered, pulled in directions and distorted into interpretations the Founding Fathers never pondered, never anointed.

Let me offer a whimsical yet telling analogy. On the last day of the Congress, moments before a vote was taken to approve the Bill of Rights for submittal to the individual states for ratification, suppose Thomas Tudor Tucker from South Carolina had stood and stated that one more amendment was necessary. Since he had to travel to Congress via roads dissecting states, to assure both him and other citizens of the United States unhindered travels, he proposed this additional Right be considered:

> *All people shall have the right to travel, unimpeded, on the paths and roads within, and among, those states of the United States.*

While I am not stating with absolute confidence that Mr. Tucker's proposal would have been added forthwith to the inventory of rights, it may well have been included because it was noncontroversial. Much as most Americans had, in their everyday life, the need to own a musket, Americans had the need to drive their wagons full of a harvest on any path or road unimpeded.

Now, dear reader, with your musket beside you on the wagon seat, let us suppose the proposed amendment from the South Carolina delegate had been included in the Bill of Rights. If so, America would now have two NRAs lobbying Congress. One, the National Rifle Association; the other, the National Racers Association. The former would be arguing the "right to bear arms" allows today's metropolitan Americans, who live in cities of concrete and brick, nearly totally devoid of grass and trees, to buy one handgun a month, or, if so preferred, an assault weapon. These Americans, who likely would not be able to find a deer in a forest, provided they could find a forest, let alone gut a deer once slain, should certainly not be disallowed from purchasing armor-piercing ammunition for their guns . . . so sayeth the NRA.

The "right to travel roads unimpeded" would, as argued by the second NRA lobbyists, allow Americans to drive their gas-guzzling sports cars at 150 miles per hour along the interstate highways unimpeded. As with assault weapons killing Americans, speeders would do the same. But as some learned student of Constitutional Law would quickly admonish, "We may not violate the wisdom of the Founding Fathers as memorialized in the Bill of Rights."

I knew the Founding Fathers. Many possessed wisdom. None possessed clairvoyant wisdom. None possessed absurd wisdom.

Since I have now broached the subject of clairvoyant wisdom, permit me to address those black-robed Americans with newly discovered clairvoyant powers. If the truth of the matter be told, to suggest that the wisdom of our Supreme Court is fallible was not a comfortable declaration for me to make. Until now I have always held my tongue, believing that only the most learned and the most competent donned the robes of our nation's highest court. Yet as I watched the inauguration of our most recent president, as I watched in startled amazement and disbelief as the chief justice, having had months to prepare, first dissected, then commingled those few words that together form the President of the United States' Oath of Office, I reconsidered.

Let me return to the First Amendment's freedom of speech and the clairvoyant powers some members of the Supreme Court claim to possess. Most recently, the nation's highest court ruled that corporations and individual Americans have the identical First Amendment rights. This quizzical ruling gutted years of standing legislation and, in atypical fashion, squashed the precedent-setting rulings of other courts.

Know with a certitude that as sure as boiling water turns to steam, we Founding Fathers did not consider the rights of corporations. Recall: The Bill of Rights was set forth to protect the basic principles of human liberty. In time, and with the application of the most painful and warped logic, I might be swayed and no longer be perplexed by the Court's recent ruling on the First Amendment rights of corporations. A statement by the Court bolstering its recent ruling, however, is the most troublesome, a statement offered in rebuttal to the dissenting members of the Court. As proffered by one Supreme Court judge in defense of the Court's ruling: "Our enterprising Founders probably would have wanted to protect corporate speech, with the possible exception of Thomas Jefferson, who favored an agrarian society."

Other than the portion of the statement addressing Mr. Jefferson's predilection for farmers, untrue. Any Founding Father would have offered only a portrait stare if the notion of corporations speaking out for themselves had been tendered. Corporations would have possessed, for me and for all of our other Founders, the same abilities to speak as trees, houses, and the horses that pulled our carriages. Thus, to give them the freedom of speech would have been nonsensical and, yes, absurd.

The Founding Fathers wrote what they wrote. They wrote it plainly. They wrote it in English.

We allowed that you could have a cup of milk; you took our cow.

—Poorer Richard's America, *September 2010*

DISTRIBUTE PRESSURE, DISTRIBUTE CONSEQUENCES

... Don't Let Them Stand Calmly By with Their Hands in Their Pockets

Before I place my thoughts of this essay to paper, let me apologize to the Amish of my dear Lancaster, Pennsylvania, and those citizens of my Philadelphia. As you might know, I was Postmaster of Philadelphia. Then, Postmaster to America; not the America you know, but the America of the Colonies. Then in the year 1785 I was elected President, today known as Governor, of Pennsylvania. This position I held for three years. A digression back to my life not needed, my pardon tendered. The Amish of Lancaster were selected for this essay to demonstrate the absurdity of an issue, an issue best brought forth by an analogy. Please, take no offense, my friendly Amish.

Imagine, if you would, that during the 1990s a most radical Amish elder, one living a calm life in Lancaster, began to preach hatred. Many young Amish men sat at his feet and listened to his teachings. He taught that those Mormons in Salt Lake City were evil Satans. He taught that they should be slain and that all those sacrificing themselves to slay Mormons would be granted both a Hooters franchise and Super Bowl tickets in the afterlife. In time Amish living in the city of Philadelphia came to hear the elder's teachings; upon considering his holy words, they offered monies to finance those who would sacrifice themselves.

Thus it came to pass that many Mormons were slain while living a peaceful existence in Salt Lake City. When the truth of the matter became known, that some Amish from Lancaster County had caused the grief, and that the Amish of Philadelphia had financed them in their attacks on the innocent Mormons, a much-angered Mayor of Salt Lake City demanded action by the Mayor of Philadelphia. With much indignation the Philadelphia Mayor responded by stating that the Amish of Philadelphia were a holy people who knew nothing of any misdeeds, and that the issue should be resolved by the people of Salt Lake City, and that no Mormons should journey to Philadelphia seeking redress of grievances, lest they offend his holy Amish constituents.

Not an acceptable response I think. Perhaps Salt Lake City's Mayor should advise the Philadelphia Mayor that his world might well spin differently if another Mormon was harmed.

If, dear reader, your mind is befuddled by this essay, think not of Mormons, but of Americans, and think not of Amish, but of those in far-off lands that live in grand palaces with great pools of oil beneath.

UNINTENDED CONSEQUENCES, FOREIGN AFFAIRS

. . . JOE THE WELDER NOW WORKS THE FRYER

For you shallow students of American History, during the 1940s a war of epic death and destruction ravaged our good Earth; more than seventy million combatants and civilians were killed during World War II. The major warring nations were the United States, Britain, and the

Soviet Union against Germany, Italy, and Japan. As the war neared its conclusion in Europe, while the forces of America and Britain rushed toward Berlin from the west and the Red Army closed on the German capital from the east, the leaders of America, Britain, the Soviet Union, and France[3] gathered to determine precisely and finally how best to administer and divide a defeated Germany, the broad outlines of their plan having been limned in earlier at summit conferences among the Big Three—the U.S., Britain, and the Soviet Union—in Casablanca and Tehran.

France, having been twice invaded and once occupied by Germany in the first half of the twentieth century, argued that Germany should be rendered a nation of farmers: no steel mills, no weapons, no standing military forces. The Soviet Union wanted serious indemnities paid, having been invaded and the eastern portion of its territory decimated by the Wehrmacht, and having lost twenty-three million of its citizens to Germany; adamant, the Soviets sought a deep and lasting retribution.

In time a finalized arrangement emerged. Germany was divided into four zones: British, French, American, and Soviet. The Soviet Zone occupied the eastern portion of Germany while America, Britain, and France assumed control of the western portion. After several years the occupiers of Germany departed and left the Germans to reestablish their own government, except the Soviets did not quite depart. Instead, they converted their zone to the

---

[3] France was not a major power, but it had a mutual defense pact with Britain before the war and was an American ally of long standing.

German Democratic Republic, a satellite country they added to several other Eastern European satellite countries they had gained suzerainty over through alleged American naiveté. The Soviets remained to administer what became the German Democratic Republic or, colloquially, East Germany. The remainder of Germany, formally the Federal Republic of Germany, colloquially known as West Germany, established a democracy left free to exercise its citizens' initiatives and energies.

With the historical scenery well built, on to the tragic play.

A few years after the end of World War II, 1947 to be more precise than less precise, I was drifting over Harvard. By this time it was a university and not a college as it was when I addressed the faculty in 1753. And it was still a college in 1775 when General Washington asked that Mr. Lynch, Mr. Harrison, and I travel to Cambridge, Massachusetts, to assist in establishing administrative order of those independent, undisciplined farmers, trappers, and merchants who, with their few muskets and tattered morale, were together, in all of their uneven patriotism, the buds of what we hoped, we prayed, would spring forth as the Continental Army. So, I did it again. Another rabbit trail of remembrance followed from the path of this essay. Forgive me.

In June 1947 I was in the shadows of Memorial Church as Secretary of State George Marshall addressed the graduating class of Harvard University. After the obligatory congratulatory phrases, Secretary Marshall turned his words to the economic plight of ravaged postwar Europe, proposing a major American aid program to "assist in the return of normal economic health to the world." His outline of American assistance that day became known as the Marshall Plan, under which $12 billion—in 1947 a billion dollars was a bigger billion than today ($1,200 bought a new car, $9,500 a house)—went to aid European countries, including West Germany, which two short years before was America's mortal foe. The Russian-controlled East Germany received no aid from its master.

Another point of World War II history: Four months after Germany surrendered, Japan collapsed under two mushroom clouds and signed an unconditional surrender on the USS *Missouri*, anchored victoriously in Tokyo Harbor. As Russia was America's ally in defeating Germany, it was also our late-war ally against Japan, and on the deck of the great battleship the Russians watched the defeated Japanese diplomats bow before signing.

Now a question for you, dear readers. If, at the brutal end of World War II, the United States, rather than helping to rebuild Japan and West Germany, had allowed the Russians to occupy all of Germany, not just East Germany, and all of Japan, how might America be different today?

While immodest of me, let me tender an answer while you ponder my question. There would be no Porsches, Toyotas, Volkswagens, Hondas, Mercedes, Nissans, BMWs, Lexuses, Audis, or any other car manufactured in Germany or Japan clogging American highways; and there wouldn't be laid-off autoworkers working the fry machine. The American automobile industry would be, today, as robust as it was in the 1950s.

Let me also tender two potential counterpoints to my premise with my response to each. First, the automobile executives of General Motors, Ford, and Chrysler have, for the past few decades, acted with an incompetence and apathy, overlaid with arrogance, not seen since Louis XVI watched comfortably, from his gold throne, the eradication of his monarchy. A well-sharpened guillotine would have served as well as the early retirement program for your automobile executives. The actions—or, better stated, the inactions—of Detroit's executives in the 1970s and 1980s were treasonous to America's manufacturing base. As Americans had waded ashore at Normandy and Iwo Jima three decades before, Germany and Japan waded ashore onto American lands to sell cars and build factories. As these foreign car manufacturers gained market share, your automobile executives made condescending comments about foreign products while leaving their offices early for tennis and drinks at the exclusive Dearborn Racquet Club.

Second counterpoint: Those PhD sages of international studies sequestered in our State Department would quickly lecture me that there was compelling geopolitical logic for America not allowing Russia to occupy all of Germany and Japan. Perhaps, but I think not.

From the 1950s through the 1990s the Soviet Union was perceived by most Americans as the greatest threat to their Country, and to democracy. I was fearful, fearful for our America, when Premier Khrushchev pounded his shoe on a desk at the United Nations and predicted Russia would bury America. A knowledgeable and prudent man could have argued that by allowing Russia to occupy all of Germany and Japan, we would have foolishly permitted our sworn enemy closer to our shores.

First point for your consideration, dear reader: between America and East Germany is 3,400 miles. If Russia held claim to all of Germany, it would have been only two hundred miles closer to our eastern boundary. Other than France being nervous, thus likely miscorking their clarets, with Russia sharing a border, no seismic geopolitical shifts. Since the closest point between Russia and America is the tip of Alaska . . . did you know that you can see Russia from Alaska? . . . Russia occupying Japan would not have moved the Communist threat any closer to the American Flag.

Yes, I know. When North Korea invaded South Korea in 1950, America would not have been able to utilize Japan to stage its military forces to push the North Koreans off South Korea's territory. If this be the truth, what would be the difference for America? American taxpayers wouldn't have had to pay for 25,000 of our troops to remain in South Korea for the past six decades, and Americans wouldn't be driving Hyundais or Kias.

To those of you who question whether the Japanese and German auto industries would have failed to flourish under Russia's communism, consider how many cars Americans have purchased from Russia, East Germany, Poland, Czechoslovakia, or any other formerly communist-controlled country.

Certainly, dear reader, the thesis of this essay was not to dissect the history and circumstances of world automobile manufacturing. Nor was it intended to rebuke those who fashioned the Marshall Plan, a plan that tempered the suffering of tens of millions of men, women, and children. Its intent was, as with Fannie and Freddie, to demonstrate that good intentions—spending billions of American taxpayer dollars to rebuild other nations—does not necessarily equate, as might a mathematical equation of certain absolutes and constants, to a favorable outcome for the nation that, at all times, we must give our first and most enthusiastic priority: our America.

THE NATIONAL DEBT DOES NOT MATTER

. . . It Does Matter

A select group of elected officials, dilettantes of fiscal policy, have asserted that annual national deficits are not relevant; America, they maintain, will find a way out of the crumbling mine shaft of debt it has dug . . . and continues to dig.

With your leave, a brief counterpoint is presented herewith. The impending death of a ten-year-old is so much more dispiriting than the impending death of a sixty-year-old. Likewise with the National Debt; anyone claiming the National Debt does not matter is not young, nor does such a person possess any understanding of his rightful obligations to those younger generations of Americans, and even to those yet-to-be-born generations. Those who claim that a $13 trillion debt does not matter were not born into even a single-trillion-dollar deficit. They were not brought into a world where, if you are now born as an American, lying next to you in your cradle is a past-due notice, advising that you already owe $42,000 as your share of the National Debt; and that you will need to pay $1,700 a year in taxes to cover the interest until the principal on that note is paid off . . . and you expected to be breast-fed?

> *If you are in a hole, stop digging.*
> —Author unknown

But even if you do stop digging—by stopping your personal spending—others will continue to dig for you; they will dig the National Debt into a deeper hole each year, and going forward each American citizen will have an ever-larger share of it to repay. The most frightful excavator digging away is the interest compounding on our National Debt with each swing of the clock's pendulum. Be ever mindful that interest never sleeps, it never tires; rather, it works away while you play and rest.

Let me show interest first as an ally, not as an enemy. Upon my death in 1790 I bequeathed the equivalent of $4,500 to the city of my birth, Boston. This money was placed into a trust that after one hundred years was worth $400,000. Of this amount, $300,000 was utilized to found the Benjamin Franklin Institute of Technology. The remaining $100,000 remained in the trust, thus compounding and growing to $5 million during the next hundred years.

Interest as your enemy, compounding on debt, not as your ally compounding on savings, is no less powerful. This fact I taught my grandchildren when I asked them to guess how much would be owed at the end of a thirty-day month if, starting with a penny the first day, one doubled the amount owed each day. Permit me to calculate the first week. Day one, 1 cent; day two, 2 cents; day three, 4 cents; day four, 8 cents; day five, 16 cents; day six, 32 cents, and day seven . . . one week . . . 64 cents.

By the end of one week a penny owed had grown to 64 pennies owed. By the thirtieth day? The answer: a frightful $5,368,709.12.[4]

Dear Americans, your National Debt not only matters; it will consume all before it.

---

[4] No, not a mistake. Please turn the page.

Penny Chart

Days	Money
I	$0.0I
2	$0.02
3	$0.04
4	$0.08
5	$0.I6
6	$0.32
7	$0.64
8	$I.28
9	$2.56
I0	$5.I2
II	$I0.24
I2	$20.48
I3	$40.96
I4	$8I.92
I5	$I63.84
I6	$327.68
I7	$655.36
I8	$I,3I0.72
I9	$2,62I.44
20	$5,242.88
2I	$I0,485.76
22	$20,97I.52
23	$4I,943.04
24	$83,886.08
25	$I67,772.I6
26	$335,544.32
27	$67I,088.64
28	$I,342,I77.28
29	$2,684,354.56
30	$5,368,709.I2

INTERNATIONAL AFFAIRS

. . . It's Just a Hundred Games of Chess, Played Concurrently

As domestic affairs were less complex in the earliest chapters of America's life, so were international affairs. In the 1700s and 1800s there was a broad delegation of world authority. Great Britain, Spain, France, Holland, Austria, and Prussia all, to some extent, exercised imperialism. They occupied and administered scores of other nations. For a world equivalent of the United Nations meeting held in 1850, say, at the Congress of Vienna, less than a dozen essential chairs for powerful nations were necessary. Today hundreds of nations, each with aspirations, needs, concerns, and agendas, clamor for equality in voice and representation on the world stage. And the vast majority, if not all, of these nations seek what is best for them, not what is best for the world. As Winston Churchill stated closer to your time than my time, people have friends; nations have interests.

For many decades I enjoyed chess. As the briefest digression, long after my death I was honored with membership in the American Chess Congress; hence, I was much as that poor lad who died of starvation only to have his friends lay loaves of bread on his tombstone. Let me rejoin. Chess is a means of mental training. To the inquisitive player, to the player who wishes to better himself, chess offers many skills of the mind and learned instincts.

i. **Foresight**, *which looks a little into the future, and considers the consequences that may attend an action; for it is continually occurring to the player, "If I move this piece, what will be the advantages or disadvantages of my new situation?"*

ii. **Circumspection**, *which surveys the whole chessboard, the scene of action, and then assesses the relations of the several pieces and situations, the dangers they are respectively exposed to . . . and*

iii. **Caution**, *not to make one's moves too hastily.*

These same skills and qualities of mind and maneuver should be well considered by those Americans who manage our Country's foreign affairs. With this analogy, however, there is a problem. Much as I had a fair chance of besting any single opponent in a game of chess, had I played against many individuals at once, a loser to most all I would have been, perhaps even to all. American leaders are not dull of mind. Playing against any one nation in world affairs, America will win. But, dear sirs and ladies, there are a hundred nations, with intelligent leaders, often schooled in the best American institutions, that are seeking to best us in their dealings with America. And they take advantage, this done by emotionally evoking America's might and wealth as a reason America should acquiesce to their needs.

There is no little enemy.
—Poor Richard's, *September 1733*

After twenty years of practicing statesmanship, and more than two hundred years of observing the same, for your consideration let me humbly set forth a few of my suggested rules and mischievous notions for conducting America's international affairs:

Rule 1. Michelle Obama was correct. Even though she believed that her husband would be a sterling President, before she acquiesced to his candidacy she sought assurances that her family, her daughters, and her home would be secure and not rendered insolvent if he committed to serving America. This should be the manner in which America conducts itself. America's first responsibility is not to better the world, but to remain solvent. When all is tranquil and secure at home, America can help others.

Rule 2. Teddy Roosevelt was also correct: "Speak softly and carry a big stick." As I observe America in its posturing with smaller nations, I have the same uneasy feeling as when I listen to modern parents attempting to control their unruly child. "Johnny, I'm not going to tell you again": This threat is played over and over until it approaches the fourth power, all the time Johnny seemingly oblivious to any need to modify his behavior. How many times can America threaten, decade after decade, a juvenile nation before America realizes that, as a child with a parent, we are being played. Better we warn once, then react if no heed is taken. One quick strike on the buttocks, a child knows the truth of a threat and modifies his behavior. Thus it be for all.

Rule 3. Remember that:

- If America is disrespectful of other nations, they will not respect us.
- If America is overly respectful of other nations, they will not respect us.
- If America tenders onto other nations financial considerations, they will merely *say* they respect us.

- If America maintains its own financial house in good repair, acts decisively in world affairs, and is respectful of other nations, they will respect us . . . and they will fear us.

Rule 4. America needs to demand reciprocity and equality of accommodations when dealing with other nations. Two decades ago, when the Nation of All Sand No Grass was threatened by a neighbor, America exercised its might to reassure and protect the Nation of All Sand No Grass. Leaders of this same Nation ask that their citizens receive special considerations when in America, and are quickly offended if they perceive the most minor slight against their All Sand religion or their No Grass culture while in our country. Yet Americans in their country are soon arrested if, in the most casual manner, any of their actions or statements are inconsistent with the doctrines and religions of that All Sand No Grass Nation. America cannot always be the accommodator, nor the apologist.

Tell me my faults, and mend your own.
                        —Poor Richard's, *December 1756*

Reciprocity and equal accommodation also need to be demanded from America's old friends, even those who provided me so many enjoyable days and memories. The country of many wine corks welcomed Americans, as many died on its soil, driving out Nazis; it welcomed billions of dollars of American aid. Yet when America asked to overfly their country in a retaliatory mission against Libya, this country of many wine corks denied permission. This be the same Libya to which the Scottish justice minister released the Lockerbie bomber, convicted of blowing up the Pan Am Boeing 747 with 270 innocent and happy American souls on board, many returning to their homes and families for Christmas, souls whose deaths were mourned by thousands of friends and relatives. The release of this bomber, if I exist another three hundred years, I will not be able to reconcile.

Rule 5. America should address citizens of the world as equals; it should not address all leaders of nations as equals. The President of the United States, by responding to trivial and inane pronouncements from leaders of nations of small shadows, aggrandizes and emboldens such leaders. If, while conducting his nation's business, the leader of a nation of a small shadow wears a uniform resplendent with self-awarded medals of no meaning, or dresses in an open shirt, as if he is an aging disco dancer, perhaps a conclusion regarding the intellect and mental health of such a leader may be drawn by the observant person.

Rule 6. When utilizing negative and demeaning terms, address such to the leaders of a nation, not to the nation. Most all peoples of all nations seek the same: a contented life, a safe home, and a healthy family. Nations are not evil; all citizens of nations are not evil. Leaders of nations may be evil.

Corn, six months from planting till eating. Fruit trees, years upon years from planting till eating. Those who manage the affairs of state tend an orchard.
—Poorer Richard's America, *September 2010*

EQUAL RIGHTS LEGISLATION

. . . Headwinds, No; Tailwinds, No

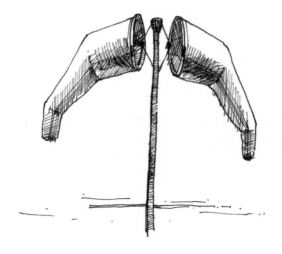

No, there should be no arbitrary impediment for any American seeking "life, liberty, and the pursuit of happiness." Almost everyone would certainly agree that each and every American citizen should enjoy equality of basic rights . . . among others, those set forth in our Bill of Rights. Thus, any proposed legislation that attempts to assure "equality" of access to human rights is worthy of passage.

With a hesitancy even greater than that with which I approached my discourse on the Second Amendment, let me address a concern of mine. My concern is equal rights legislation that mandates various promotions based not alone on merit, but on cultural considerations. Clearly, I understand that "considerations" on hiring must be equitable; the Rooney Rule dictates that NFL teams must interview members of minorities for coaching positions, but it does not mandate that a member of a minority must be hired.

The problem, I believe, is not awarding a minority a job over another, or a merit increase over another; it is taking away a job or a merit increase from another. One of a person's most basic needs, a most emotional need, is to be a good provider to a loving family. When a position is awarded, in full or in part, because of cultural or ethnic considerations, it may be argued that something of value was taken from another citizen. And while the history of a minority may show a century of denied rights, and exploitation in the most harsh and inhuman manner, as debts do not flow from father to son, neither should guilt or retribution.

If any of my remarks are callous and without merit, I apologize to those I have offended.

None know the unfortunate, and the fortunate do not know themselves.
—Poor Richard's, *February 1747*

Essay counterpoint: This essay is built on the premise that discrimination no longer lurks in businesses, and thus, there is no need to pay for past debts. Perhaps prejudice hides in the folds of America's fabric, doing so by being more polite than decades before. Thus, while today's discrimination may wear soft silk gloves, its firm grip may still restrain.

Each snapping turtle argument has a soft underbelly.
—Poorer Richard's America, *September 2010*

SOCIAL SURPLUS

. . . Pyramids, Highways, or Nothing

Five thousand years ago the Pharaoh Menes united the peoples of the Upper Nile and the Lower Nile. Two small digressions: Since the Nile flows to the north, the upstream portion is referred to as the Upper Nile, even though it is hundreds of miles south of where the Nile commingles its waters with those of the Mediterranean Sea. Thus the Lower Nile is the Upper Nile . . . unless one is standing on one's head. Second digression: Quite pleased I am to speak of Menes, who is close to five thousand years old, so weary have I become of addressing those more than two hundred years younger than me.

Having united the peoples of Egypt into a more efficient single nation, Menes began the first national program in the history of mankind. To direct the waters of the Nile, when they overflowed their banks each year, Menes ordered the building of canals to irrigate and render fertile those lands that had never tasted water. A decade later, with the project complete, Egypt's population prospered and expanded with an abundance of crops.

For the peoples of Egypt to lay down whatever they were doing and dig canals required a social surplus, a social surplus being the positive difference between what a nation is producing and what it consumes. Or, if the nation has climbed up the evolutionary chain of nations, the positive difference between its government's inflow of tax revenues and its outflow of expenditures.

The result of Menes applying Egypt's social surplus to digging a network of canals was to render Egypt more productive. Thus, in time, even greater social surpluses were available for national programs. Pharaohs of following generations, with self-esteem deficits, built pyramids, monuments to themselves, which consumed social surplus but did nothing that offered the Egyptian peoples advantages, as did the canals. Let me correct myself. A few thousand years later in your world of today, the pyramids serve as a centerpiece to Egypt's tourism business; as you would say, better late . . . five thousand years . . . than never.

So then, how may a nation best allocate its social surplus? The answer is, the same way as Menes did: Build the equivalent of the canals of Egypt. For you, dear citizens, that means building infrastructure: interstate highways, pipelines, high-speed railways, bridges, hydroelectric generation plants and power grids, and other projects that have lasting benefit. Other uses of social surplus can include a strong military, to allow a people to sleep safely; and a journey to the moon, to allow citizens to stand proudly.

Today America has many social surplus programs, programs that require a broad and deep stream of revenue, and a resultant surplus. Regrettably, there is no federal surplus. Hence, America has social deficit programs. And many of these programs have no residual benefit . . . they are not building for the future of America or its people. Rather, many programs only create short-term benefits for a few years; too often, these programs merely generate activity and temporary jobs to maintain the status quo and garner political support: building an airport in a congressional district that will never be served by a commercial carrier . . . such airport christened with the name of the Congressman that pulled monies from the Federal Treasury to fund the project.

Unlike the Pharaoh Menes's enlightened leadership of Egypt five thousand years ago, America has the "inside-out worst" of no social surplus and a national leadership borrowing money to fund programs that fail to leave even an ash of benefit to the taxpayer—the only lasting legacy being interest the taxpayer must pay on the funds the government borrowed and burned. Better America builds pyramids, even if they do require a few thousand years to pay dividends.

HEALTH-CARE REFORM

. . . I'D RATHER CHARGE BUNKER HILL

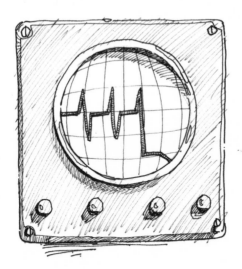

After a long year of your sensory receptors being rubbed raw with continuous shrill warnings of death panels, back-alley abortions, and other ends of your lives as presently enjoyed, most Americans became numb to legitimate health-care debate and pleaded for either a truce or surrender. What they received was capitulation.

While offering some relief to your citizens, in its final mutation the recently enacted health-care legislation is both anemic and misengineered. It is, however, a perfectly crafted representation of the vested interests of corporations . . . excuse me . . . of those key components of today's health-care industry. And while Congress and the White House may be chastised for allowing health-care legislation to be shaped by the pillars of the status quo, the real problem lies elsewhere. That elsewhere being close to a total misunderstanding of health-care fundamentals.

This cannot be, you say. For a time months longer than that frigid Valley Forge winter, America's television and radio waves were saturated with talking heads and indignant legislators targeting health care's most egregious offenders: insurance companies that deny claims; dastardly for-profit HMOs; greedy, uncaring physicians; Stone Age medical records systems; and the Sons of Satan, malpractice attorneys. Acid comments about rampant Medicare fraud and illegal aliens clogging the ERs filled any gaps in airtime. Are these problems for your American health-care industry? Certainly. But none is the key driver of health-care inflation. So then, pray tell, what are the most basic health-care fundamentals?

Fundamental Number One, there is no "real" health insurance, so do not concern yourself with the extra tests and paper medical records. Health insurance disappeared years ago. True insurance is the concept of a large group of people pulling from their purses a few dollars to cover the cost of a potential catastrophic event that may befall only the most unlucky. When one buys homeowner's insurance, it's not with the expectation that one's house will burn to the ground. To the contrary, the majority of today's Americans with health insurance expect to utilize it; well-baby care, eye exams, wart removals, and, perhaps, a prescription for Prozac. If homeowner's insurance had been on the same evolutionary path as health insurance for the past three decades, today's homeowner's insurance would pay for repairing furnaces, applications of crabgrass killer, cleaning gutters, and checking the fireplace flue for ash buildup . . . a colonoscopy for the house.

True health insurance was strangled by unions and state insurance commissioners who, bless their hearts, kept negotiating and mandating more and more comprehensive benefits . . . cleaning the gutters, so to speak. Thus, many self-employed American workers cannot afford the all-inclusive health plans mandated by legislation. What they need—low-cost catastrophic health insurance (true insurance)—is sitting next to the spotted owl. Yet another example, I regret to inform, of dire unintended consequences—unaffordable high premiums—flowing from well-intended, all-inclusive, comprehensive health coverage.

Fundamental Number Two, and perhaps the most important: If you wish to be frugal and save money, you can switch from butter to margarine, but you can only make the economic move once. Same, dear citizens, with health care. By miracle of miracles, if next month the just-enacted health-care legislation squeezed out each and every inefficiency in your health-care delivery system; lowered Medicaid reimbursement levels; caused insurance companies, HMOs, and pharmaceutical firms to forfeit their profits; retrained malpractice attorneys as Vegas pit bosses; and transmitted medical records instantaneously through Bill Gates's personal computer, health-care costs would drop, perhaps up to 25 percent. Certainly good news for Americans. Of course, it won't happen, but certainly it would be good news.

Now for the somber news. Once aggregate health-care costs ratcheted down 25 percent, they would resume their steady march upward at 7 to 9 percent a year. In three short years America's health-care expenditures would be painfully back to where we are today . . . then climbing from there.

While erasing three years of health-care inflation would certainly be met with rousing cheers, it's the never-ending, always-rising slope of health-care costs that is our greatest challenge. Americans, and their leaders, need to understand why the slope is relentless and steep. Drumroll please . . . enter the heart and brain.

Two human organs, the heart and brain, cause the most angst for health-care policy makers. Let us begin with the heart. Every few weeks the local news covers a human interest story along the lines of half a score of concerned firemen and policemen huddled around under a tree, pondering how best to retrieve a stranded cat high above.

While the human heart has immense compassion, it does not possess a calculating capability. *Homo sapiens* are quite prepared to expend $1,000 of municipal labor costs to rescue a meowing feline. A feline similar to the dozens of others that another municipal employee efficiently euthanizes at the county animal shelter each week. This very same irrational heart drives humans to demand boundless care for their loved ones. Americans are not Spock-like. There is no price sensitivity to the love of family . . . especially if someone else is paying. The heart expects, demands, the best and most technically advanced care available.

Technically advanced care—did I just obliquely reference the brain, the second culprit in rising health-care costs? The human brain, while acting bizarrely at times, usually while under the undue influence of the only organ in our body's southern hemisphere, is masterful in contriving technical solutions to the most daunting challenges. Thus, percolating human brains continually conjure up new health-care products and services, and even if only offering a sliver of benefit, these innovations are quickly marketed to, and embraced by, medical providers: a $1.6 million robotic surgical instrument or a $400,000 open MRI for claustrophobic patients, to name just a few.

Classic retorts to the above appear valid; ever-expanding health-care technology serves to better diagnose and cure people, thus limiting medical costs in the long run. As someone said, "A beautiful theory is often broken by one ugly fact." For every new technology of unquestionable benefit, there are scores of others with only fuzzy subjective value. And even if a new technology is a silver bullet—all lung cancers immediately diagnosed and cured—aggregate health expenditures would not drop by the "cost" of treating lung cancer. Americans who would have succumbed to lung cancer will only live to suffer a heart attack, an aneurysm, or twenty years of acute dementia. Scan the obituaries, dear citizens; people don't die of old age, they die after long illnesses.

But enough of my ramblings. A specific example, if I may. Let us suppose that one of those magnificently intelligent—both in their research and marketing—pharmaceutical manufacturers develops a miracle pill. A small green pill. If an individual, with death approaching, takes this pill, he will live another year. One pill, another year of life . . . it's an absolute. Two pills, three pills, still only one year; thus, no need to take more than one pill.

Now let us consider the following chart:

Cost of New Pill In Dollars	If the Patient Pays, Will He Accept Pill?	If the Federal Government Pays, Will Patient Accept Pill?
5	Yes	Yes
50	Yes	Yes
500	Yes	Yes
1,000	Yes	Yes
5,000	Yes	Yes
25,000	?	Yes
100,000	?	Yes
500,000	?	Yes

Sorrowful reader, America already possesses the magical little green pill. It is in the form of the last year of your life, when many Americans enjoy their twilight months in a hospital with soft breezes from a ventilator flowing painfully down their throat; well-prepared meals, pre-chewed and served through a feeding tube; and, as a poised waiter removing porcelain china after a fine meal, a diaper collecting table scraps. (Recall the essay on Sir Pringle cutting the heads off the Mosquito Hawks to extend their lives.)

He's the best physician that knows the worthlessness of most medicines.
> —Poor Richard's, *September 1733*

The wondrous . . . and it truly is wondrous . . . medical technology of your America allows life to be extended in most medical calamities. But the cost is nontrivial. End-of-life care in a hospital is easily $100,000 to $200,000 a month. And remember the balloons floating over Paris in 1783: the more people in the basket, the bigger the balloon . . . tax. Billions of dollars paid by the Federal Government, your Medicare, for those last months of life must be funded by taxes. Taxes paid by you, the American citizens.

So then, if we assume one in three Americans will spend their last months being drawn and quartered in a hospital, at a cost of $300,000, on average each American will need to pay $100,000 in taxes to fund the expense. And the $300,000 end-of-life-care cost is not fixed; it will increase as medical technology performs more and more wondrous feats.

So should the hospital patient, perhaps an elderly widow, with tubes in most of her orifices, incur $300,000 of medical charges to live another three months?

If there were no Medicare, and if the patient had $300,000 in a savings account accumulated over twenty years of diligent saving, and was conscious and able to put forth her wishes, she might well elect to kiss her daughter a loving good-bye and end her life in dignity, thus leaving the $300,000 for her grandchildren's education. Likely, her daughter would tearfully concur.

If Medicare was paying for the last months of the widow's life at a cost of $300,000, and even if the failing widow asked to sleep her last sleep in dignity, her daughter may well plead . . . "Doctor, whatever it takes, please, please, the best care available."

Sirs and ladies, that most human plea above being the reason for never-ending, always-expanding health-care costs.

HEALTH-CARE REFORM, DEUX

. . . Reform Thyself

As best I can estimate, close to 300 million Americans brush their teeth each day. This commitment to healthy teeth is made without benefit of public service announcements, warnings on candy bars, or tax incentives for the purchase of toothbrushes. And for certain, no government representative appears to brush your teeth for you; it is your responsibility. Why only teeth? Shouldn't the heart, the liver, and the lungs . . . sorry, Mr. President, I do know you are trying . . . deserve the same personal commitment by Americans?

While most Americans can't speak two languages, Americans do possess more than a fair amount of common sense. You don't need labels on fast foods or employers to build exercise facilities; in your hearts you know the problem. In addition to brushing their teeth, Americans need to eat less and walk more.

When 5 percent of the population puts themselves at risk for diabetes, heart disease, high blood pressure, and lower back pain . . . I won't even mention the knees . . . their ambivalence (a euphemism) toward good health can be absorbed in the health-care premiums of others. When 30 percent of the population is ambivalent, America's health-care budget first will tilt, then fall with a most heavy thud.

To lengthen thy life, lessen thy meals.
—Poor Richard's, *June 1733*

DEPARTMENT OF DEFENSE
... THOSE WHO FIGHT, THOSE WHO
PURCHASE

It certainly is a true statement: I never served as a soldier in America's military. When I laid my signature on the Declaration of Independence I was not a young man; at seventy years of age I was far older than most sleeping in the graveyards of Philadelphia. By evoking the attributes of a self-crowned expert—an expert often being a person who has never participated in the matter on which he so knowingly advises others—I did take it upon myself to author a letter to Major General Lee in February 1776 on the preference of bow and arrows to firearms in skirmishes among soldiers. I wrote as follows:

- *A man may shoot as truly with a bow as with a common musket;*
- *He can discharge four arrows in the time of charging and discharging one bullet;*
- *His object is not taken from his view by the smoke of his own side;*
- *A flight of arrows seen coming upon them terrifies and disturbs the enemy's attention to his business; and*
- *Bows and arrows are more easily provided everywhere than muskets and ammunition.*

Any one of the many oil paintings depicting our country's struggle during the long Revolutionary War would reveal, even to the most casual observer, that my pleading was not acted upon by either Major General Lee or by our great General George Washington. If my advice had been followed, George Washington would only be noted in British history books, referenced under a discussion of traitors. The General's name wouldn't appear in the chronicles of American history; there would be no America.

Nevertheless, I am not deterred. With my ego bandaged, and with the same resolve America's militia displayed after its first losses to the Redcoats, permit me to continue with an essay regarding military affairs.

For your consideration, let me proffer that today there are two militaries serving America. One is the 1.5 million men and women of the U.S. Army, Navy, Air Force, Marines, and Coast Guard who go, for the benefit of 300 million Americans, into harm's way. Overworked and underpaid, most willingly place themselves in danger while asking their families to suffer the hardships of worry and loneliness. These Americans in uniform serve our America and, I am proudful to say, *are* our America.

The second of the two militaries resides comfortably in the five-sided monolith a mile from the Virginia bank of the Potomac River, directly across from that memorial to my friend of so many events and heavy moments, Thomas Jefferson. In this five-sided building a never-ending game of musical chairs is played by those of lower ranks seeking higher ranks. With each promotion, less likely the next promotion, until only the most capable (capable at what?) reach the highest ranks.

Let me single out the Pentagon leadership as the target (sounds military) of my critique. Many Americans are enamored with technology, more so for males. Certainly I was; I spent a fair portion of a fortnight determining how best to kill a turkey with electricity, rather than merely swinging a well-directed hatchet.

America's military leadership is enamored with technology, a technology that those smiling faces in your family picture pay for. And this infatuation with technology is nurtured, encouraged, and prodded by those defense contractors who strategically (again, military-sounding) employ thousands, yes, thousands, of retired military officers to market aircraft, missiles, and great steel ships to those in the military . . . many of whom themselves are soon to retire and seek employment in the defense industry.

> *Don't ask a barber if you need a haircut.*
> —Author unknown

For those of you who think the above quote too Old World folksy, your President Eisenhower, a former general of the highest distinction, warned as he departed the White House on a cold January day in 1961:

> *Beware of the military-industrial complex.*
> —Dwight D. Eisenhower

Is having the most technologically advanced weapons necessary? Sometimes. The questions are, what can America afford, and are the most technologically advanced weapons the ones America needs to fight today's wars? Almost two decades ago no less than your Colin Powell, a former Chairman of the Joint Chiefs of Staff, stated that America often arms itself to fight the wrong wars.

By your leave, one example: America possesses a mighty armada of jet fighters: seven hundred F-15s, thirteen hundred F-16s, and a thousand F-18s. These aircraft cost the American taxpayer between $25 and $50 million per plane. After years of laborious analysis, the Pentagon selected Lockheed Martin to manufacture the F-22, heralded as the world's most advanced fighter. A thousand were to be manufactured for America and its allies.

Somehow, as aircraft always do when hatched as a chicklet in the five-sided building, the price, as the F-22 might do with its afterburners, lit, and kept climbing; when it reached $350 million per plane, yes, per plane, the program was canceled after only 180 were purchased. In their explanation to Congress of burning a few tens of billions of dollars on the F-22, Pentagon dwellers reassured Congress that the newly ordered F-35, which would amazingly be able to hover in flight, at $50 million each would be a more-capable aircraft than the F-22. Sorry to advise that in the past ten fortnights, the forecast price has risen to $135 million . . . and its afterburners have yet to be lit.

In the Air Force's defense, the airplane as a conveyance has only been known to man for 107 years—perhaps not sufficient time to establish a costing model. Boats constructed by man have been floating right-side up for more than five thousand years, adequate time to understand the principles of ship design . . . one might think. The Coast Guard's Island Class Cutter, which possessed an array of electronics that were dazzling to behold, when recently launched was found to be structurally unsound. The crew got wet feet, and the Cutter program was canceled after hundreds of millions of dollars in expenditures.

As with our militia of 1776, it is the troops of today who carry the burden of fighting. Most are enlisted men and women, most on meager pay. For the cost of two F-22s, three hundred thousand enlisted service members at the bottom of the pay chart could receive $2,300 more a year. Or, for the cost of a single F-22, armor plate could have been put on each and every American vehicle in one of those countries of All Sand No Grass.

Does our America need a strong military? Certainly; I misspoke. Certainly, I believe. But "remaining strong" is not, as you would say, a "hall pass" to shred tens of billions of dollars on the technologically dazzling programs being marketed by defense contractors. America has the might to eradicate the planet Earth several times over, such power is resident in cruise missiles, bombers, and submarines. America must spend military dollars on the wars it knows it will fight; those wars it does fight.

> *We must be strong militarily, but beyond a certain point military strength can become a national weakness.*
>
> —Dwight D. Eisenhower

I humbly suggest for your consideration: better boots, armor plating, and housing allowances for soldiers and sailors; less dividends to the defense contractor shareholders.

*   *   *

Permit me to address those attributes of wars in which America was victorious, and attributes of those wars where victory was elusive and seemingly unattainable. Before such a discussion, a clarification:

In the first sentence of this essay I stated that I had never served in America's military. An attorney representing me would most assuredly attest that this claim is factually correct; however, anyone who knew me in 1747 would offer a knowing wink. Yes, I did serve—not in America's military, but in Pennsylvania's militia, formed to thwart the aggressions of France and Spain. No, this previous indictment is not a statement of precise happenings; it was not the military of these nations that threatened, but rather French and Spanish privateers that plundered small towns along the Delaware River. To this end, defending towns and villages, I stood my post at defensive batteries. But, before another sentence is written, let me be most candid: never an enemy seen, never a shot fired, never a single moment of my life in any way threatened. The only enemies encountered were poor food, cold lodgings, and boredom, and even these inconveniences lasted only a few short weeks. Quickly I moved from defensive batteries to a quartermaster's charge; I organized a lottery, and secured pledges that financed the purchase of much-needed artillery from England.

Now, to America's wars: America's courage and energy, with an unwavering commitment to a worthy cause, has brought many victories to our armies and our nation. Each of America's victories was accompanied by the reverse broken-mirror image of another's defeat. General O'Hara (General Cornwallis slept in) in 1781 at Yorktown; eighty-four years later, General Lee at Appomattox; Germany, on a French railway coach in 1918; again, in 1945, in Reims, France; and Japan, bowed in disgrace on the deck of the *Missouri* in Tokyo Bay, also in 1945.

While each of America's broken and defeated foes possessed many common attributes, allow me to set before you only two for your consideration. Each of America's defeated enemies wore uniforms, and each defeated military took direction from an organized and formal governing body. Hence, by clothing (uniforms), the individual enemy being fought was made known to the American warrior; and once America's armies had beaten an enemy into despair and defeat, there was a national governing body that could ponder the merits of surrender and, if such action was deemed prudent, execute a surrender with a victorious America.

If we reflect back on those wars where America did not achieve a resounding victory during the past half-century, two observations: The enemy wore the clothes of civilians rather than uniforms; and they were not soldiers of a nation, but rather soldiers of a belief—a belief that may have had a hierarchical structure, but no sovereign national structure. Hence, there was no government organ that might have sought compromise with America.

To conclude my observations concerning American wars won, and those not, let me tender two excerpts from correspondence written long ago. The first is from a letter written in 1776 by me to a British friend, Joseph Priestley, this letter posted to bring to his startled attention the cost of waging war thousands of miles from the shores of England:

> Britain, at the expense of three millions, has killed 15 Yankees this campaign, which is £20,000 a head . . . From these data a mathematical head will easily calculate the time and expense necessary to kill us all.

The following is an excerpt from a British Redcoat's letter of 1777:

We march in rigid order of four columns, twelve men each. In front of us rebels yelling and running as a mob as we march down a road in orderly pursuit. Drawn forward till the road into a forest, then a single shot from the dark behind a stand of trees and a scream of pain, and we are one less. March forward and another shot and another scream. Rebels do not stand and fight; they hide and shoot ball after ball into our flesh while they risk not a drop of blood. At night we tend the wounded and bury the dead and eat hard black bread. The rebels return to their farms, wives, children, and stewed chicken.

I ask, dear reader—if America takes on the role of the British in these excerpts, could the notions, the messages, the conclusions to be drawn from the above two paragraphs, written over two hundred and thirty years ago, fit well the profile of America's wars of elusive victory? I think, perhaps, yes. If so, does such an affirmative answer suggest the prudence of today's military strategies?

LAW OF BIG NUMBERS

. . . As You Would Say, Strange Rangers

It is the Law of Big Numbers. The greater the number, or occurrences, of an item or event, the wider the range of variations; the greater the spread in extremes. One person, one height. A million persons, some extremely diminutive citizens, some quite tall people, and many, many in between. So it be with personalities and intellect. The greater the number of people, the farther out the out-liers . . . did I just write "out the outliers"? Sounds almost like a double negative, which in proper King's English is certainly a no-no.

The point of the above rambling is that Americans should not be disheartened. With 300 million citizens there will be, by necessity, some extremes . . . the Law of Big Numbers. A few Americans will act in most bizarre and frightening manners at times. And know that with 300 million *Homo sapiens*, even a small sliver of the total is many, one-hundredth of 1 percent, no less than thirty thousand. And America's media, a media always thirsty for a quick drink of controversy or imagined adventure, is poised and ready—"We interrupt this program"—to give those most-bizarre few media coverage several magnitudes greater than the weight of the event.

So, dear Americans, those most absurd and fanciful Americans under the magnifying glass of media are truly only a few being distorted to appear of a greater voice. They are not a true slice of Americana. Do not lose heart. However . . .

Within the population of 300 million Americans there resides a smallest fraction of a percent of those with little reasoning and the most malleable of minds; some believe Elvis lives, others visit with spacemen from distant planets. A warning, if I may, to those who speak with a national voice, a voice carried by radio and television, a voice that carries to that smallest portion of Americans with the most malleable minds—minds that may misinterpret poorly con-structed analogies as patriotic calls to action. I ask that you do not suggest "reload and take aim," or any other imagined declaration of hurtful action. Once acted upon, it is too late to claim that no harm was intended. I ask, as a Founding Father of a democracy, a democracy driven by the collective will of the people, I ask that we do not suggest, in any manner, no matter how innocently intended, no matter how absurd to most—I ask that we not speak to any action that, if taken, would cause our flag to hang limp and not wave proudly.

BRANCHES OF GOVERNMENT

. . . LEGISLATIVE, EXECUTIVE, JUDICIAL, AND CORPORATE

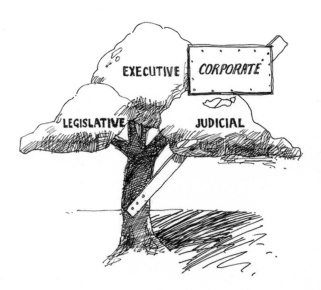

One of my previous essays set forth the premise that an elected representative in America's Congress has competing or, more harshly stated, conflicting considerations clamoring to sway his vote . . . what is best for his state, best for his constituency, best for his party, and what may be best for his reelection. While the last consideration, best for reelection, would appear to be personal, and thus not worthy of even a moment's reflection by a morally erect people's representative, it could be argued otherwise. To serve one's constituency, one needs to remain in office; hence, an elected official may not vote his patriotic heart on a matter that, because of some emotional volatility with his constituents, might cause him to surrender his position as their able (in his eyes, certainly) representative.

But in a few instances, not many, but a few, elected representatives take actions for personal gain; a gain in their own net worth. Thus, they shape legislation in a manner that is neither the absolute best for their state, constituents, country, or reelection, but rather what is most accommodating to that industry in which, or from which, they seek to personally benefit. The worst of it is not the money the elected official earns once he leaves Congress—his stipend, to put it kindly; no, the worst of it is rather the cost to taxpayers of a thousand times a thousand for each dollar they appropriate to the favored industry. The ill-advised and ill-begotten programs these members of Congress contrive through the legislature survive the member's time in office, thus becoming an indelible drain on America's Treasury.

Allocate a moment to read Article 36 of my dear Pennsylvania's Constitution.

> As every freeman to preserve his independence, (if without a sufficient estate) ought to have some profession, calling, trade, or farm, whereby he may honestly subsist, there can be no necessity for, nor use in establishing offices

*of profit, the usual effects of which are dependence and
servility unbecoming freemen, in the possessors and expect-
ants; faction, contention, corruption, and disorder among
the people.*

The spirit of those words above does not at all times
frame the actions of your Congress. I hasten to note that
I wrote "at all times." Many in Congress vote their patriotic heart; they vote their duty. But at other times, events,
personalities, and mountains of lucre conspire to create a
Devil's whirlwind of personal opportunity. What I will lay
out for you is the truth of such a matter; some might com-
plain that this American stain is a cousin, if not a brother,
to Benedict Arnold's betrayal. Consider now these few
brief but painfully salient facts:

- America's Drug Industry is large, $225 billion . . .
  yes, merely for pills. This industry is profitable,
  grizzly bear strong, and ruthless in protecting its
  earnings.
- The Drug Industry allocates more than $100 mil-
  lion a year to lobby Congress. Another few tens of
  millions are provided as campaign contributions.
- In 2003 Medicare drug legislation was drafted, and
  then passed, to provide drug benefits to Medicare
  recipients—elderly Americans. Again, these drugs
  are paid for by those smiling faces in your family
  picture.
- The drug manufacturers of America hired over
  three hundred lobbyists, more than one lobbyist
  for each two members of Congress, to influence
  the 2003 Medicare drug legislation.

- In addition to hired arm-twisters, drug manufacturers contributed great piles of dollars to the campaigns of a cadre of key members of Congress.
- Upon passage of the 2003 Medicare drug legislation, the Chairman of the House Committee overseeing Medicare announced he would be leaving
  politics to work for the Drug Industry for a quite
  handsome compensation, $2 million a year (per-
  haps he was to perform clinical research, assisting
  Sir Pringle in removing the heads of Mosquito
  Hawks).

*Sell not virtue to purchase wealth, nor liberty to
purchase power.*

—Poor Richard's, *May 1738*

Now consider one more fact that may well render you
nauseated: The few million dollars in compensation this
gentleman gathered into his waistcoat pocket was only a
small gratuity paid to the driver of the getaway car, a getaway car speeding from our National Treasury.

The Federal Government is the largest purchaser of
drugs in all the United States; in fact, in all the world. For
Medicaid, poor folks, your government obtains the lowest
price possible when purchasing drugs. Your government
has been obtaining these discounts for decades. Thus, one
might assume the drug program for Medicare recipients
would also benefit from the same bulk-purchasing power
as Medicaid. No, sorrowful reader.

The Medicare drug legislation that was so carefully crafted in 2003 by those leaving government, and those receiving campaign contributions from . . . well, you may surmise who . . . includes a clause that forbids—yes, forbids—Medicare to use its bulk-purchasing power to negotiate low drug prices. This artificial and illogical restraint means that an employer offering health insurance to his ten employees at his auto body shop in Fresno will likely pay the same amount for a bottle of pills as your government in Washington when they buy the same bottles of pills for forty million Medicare beneficiaries.

You ask, How can this be? Let me answer with another question: What do American corporations expect in return for the wagonloads of lobbying fees they pay each year?

Let me wander back 250 years to Professor Alexander Tytler of Edinburgh, Scotland. While, as I recounted in my essay on prejudice, I knew of Professor Hazlitt of Glasgow, a Scottish intellect of no small measure, never did I have the pleasure of meeting Professor Tytler of Edinburgh, another intellect of the same brilliant period. But his insightful and fearful writings I do know well. In one of his many essays, he prophesied that:

> A democracy is always temporary in nature: it simply cannot exist as a permanent form of government. A democracy will continue to exist up until the time the voters discover they can vote themselves generous gifts from the public treasury. From that moment on the majority always vote for the candidates who promise the most benefits from the public treasury, with the result that every democracy will finally collapse due to loose fiscal policy.

Those ominous words were written more than two centuries ago. That is, two centuries before America's $13 trillion debt. Just as America's Founding Fathers did not anticipate that the highest court of our land would rule that corporations had the right of free speech, Professor Tytler did not, could not, anticipate that not only would citizens clamor for monies from a democracy's treasury, but so too would mighty corporations . . . corporations of a size unimaginable two hundred years ago.

Our government must dig deep and wide moats around America's Treasury. To survive, America must expel Corporate America, and its paid agents, from the streets of Washington and the halls of Congress. As to how, my last essay will discuss a solution for your consideration.

LOVE AND MARRIAGE

. . . Best of Luck

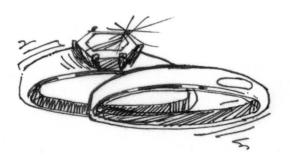

Transportation, communication, medical care, styles, morality—all together, more change since I departed two centuries ago than is possible to imagine. Love and marriage, another story . . . it is as if I never left. Rest assured, dear passionate reader, the tensions, attractions, and mysteries remain the same between the strong and the sweet. Thus, this essay is merely a compilation of those words printed in *Poor Richard's Almanacks* of long ago.

A house without woman & Firelight, is like a body without soul or sprite.

A good Wife lost is God's gift lost.

Good Women are like STARS in darkest Night,
Their Virtuous Actions shining as a Light
To guide their ignorant Sex, which oft times fall,
And falling oft, turns diabolical.
Good Women sure are Angels on the Earth,
Of those good Angels we have had a Dearth;
And therefore all you Men that have good Wives,
Respect their Virtues equal with your Lives.

One good Husband is worth two good Wives; for the scarcer things are, the more they're valued.

She that falls in love with herself, will have no Rivals.

Time was my spouse and I could not agree,
Striving about superiority:
The text which saith that man and wife are one,
Was the chief argument we stood upon:
She held, they both one woman should become;
I held they should be man, and both but one.
Thus we contended daily, but the strife
Could not be ended, till both were one Wife.

Where there's Marriage without Love, there will be Love without Marriage.

Some of our Sparks to London town do go
Fashions to see, and learn the World to know;
Who at Return have nought but these to show,
New Wig above, and new Disease below.

Keep your eyes wide open before marriage, half shut afterwards.

Sam's Wife provok'd him once; he broke her Crown,
The Surgeon's Bill amounted to Five Pound;
This Blow (she brags) has cost my Husband dear,
He'll ne'er strike more. Sam chanc'd to over-hear.
Therefore before his Wife the Bill he pays,
And to the Surgeon in her Hearing says:
Doctor, you charge Five Pound, here e'en take Ten,
My Wife may chance to want your Help again.

Good wives and good plantations are made by good husbands.

Good Death, said a Woman, for once be so kind
To take me, and leave my dear Husband behind,
But when Death appear'd with a sour Grimace,
The Woman was dash'd at his thin hatchet Face;
So she made him a Courts'y, and modestly sed,
If you come for my Husband, he lies there in Bed.

Epitaph on a Scolding Wife by her Husband:
Here my poor Bridget's Corpse doth lie, she is at
rest,—*and so am I.*

When Man and Woman die, as Poets sung,
His Heart's the last part moves, her last, the tongue.

Luke, on his dying Bed, embrac'd his Wife,
And begg'd one Favour: Swear, my dearest Life,
Swear, if you love me, never more to wed,
Nor take a second Husband to her Bed.
Anne dropt a Tear. You know, my dear, says she,
Your least Desires have still been Laws to me;
But from this Oath, I beg you'd me excuse;
For I'm already promis'd to your friend.

My humble apologies. I misspoke. I erred. While a well-contrived and a well-kept marriage is no less wonderful, nor less mysterious, since I took my leave, and while men have not changed their ways, women have changed ever so much since Poor Richard spoke of love and marriage. I erred again. It is America that changed, molded itself around women. Their intellect was always there; but America has given . . . no, another error . . . women have fought for those artificial, invisible constraints to be broken. So from the foggy distant past, let me be a voice of one offering a heartfelt and most genuine, and long past-due, apology.

KEYNESIAN ECONOMICS—
EFFECTIVE?
. . . DIPS, YES; SPIRALS, NO

Economics was a science—should I say art?—that I did not study or otherwise ponder. I did, however, during my forays to Scotland in 1759, have the pleasure of a few short walks and several long conversations with Adam Smith, who several years later authored *The Wealth*

of Nations, in which, I am pleased to note, he felt agreeable to reference my population extrapolation calculations. In his classic economic treatise, first printed in that remarkable year of 1776, Mr. Smith wrote of the "invisible hand" that guides free markets to produce the socially optimal amount of goods and services. This theory was vehemently attacked seventy-five years later in Marx's *The Communist Manifesto*. If economics is neither a science nor an art, but rather a game, the present score would appear to be Smith, 1, Marx, 0. Alas, the game is not over.

Allow me to arc forward from Edinburgh's Mr. Smith to another notable free-enterprise economist, one born closer to your birth date than mine. John Maynard Keynes was an imposing intellectual statue, chiseled, shaped, and polished by the scholarship of Cambridge University, at its King's College. In 1936, having observed the Great Depression of the early thirties—America's unemployment rate an agonizing 25 percent—Keynes wrote *The General Theory of Employment, Interest, and Money*, most often referred to as the General Theory. This book, and other writings of Keynes, proposed that governments could make less hurtful the downward cycles of their nation's economy by initiating aggressive monetary and fiscal actions, both actions serving to cause monies to be spent on goods and services, thereby stimulating the economy by the mystical power of the "multiplier effect."

In regard to monetary policy, Keynes counseled that a government should take action to drive down interest rates, thus encouraging consumers to "buy by borrowing" (which almost sounds like a limerick I would repeat to my grandchildren). Fiscal policy, the second Keynesian antidote to a lethargic economy, proposed either the lowering of taxes—allowing citizens to retain a greater portion of their wages, which would then be available to purchase goods and services—or, alternatively, the government spending tax dollars, or borrowed dollars (perhaps from the nation that in 2011 will be celebrating the Year of the Rabbit), to build dams, bridges, or highways, thus stimulating the economy with the purchase of goods and services.

Simply stated, Keynes advised governments to throw coal into their nations' economic furnaces—to put dollars, directly or indirectly, into the purses of a nation's army of consumers.

And, since I mentioned the multiplier effect, permit me to attempt an explanation. This refers to the notion that a single new dollar spent in the economy will result in several dollars' worth of economic activity. An example, if I may: Suppose that your government pays a long-unemployed carpenter to frame the footings for a highway ramp; the carpenter then spends a portion of his newly earned wages at a gas station, grocery store, shoe store, and liquor store. In turn, the proprietors of these businesses have a few dollars of greater income, allowing each of them to go to the liquor store and buy an extra six-pack. I do trust, thirsty reader, that you now comprehend well the multiplier effect: an ale for everyone.

Recalling that I did not choose to study the art of economics, perhaps the reasons become clear when considering the following formula that ever so precisely determines a Keynesian model's economic equilibrium point:

$$PE = C_o + c(1\text{-}t)Y + I^P + G + NX$$

PE corresponds to "planned expenditures." I assume no slight will be harbored if I do not expound upon the import of the other terms. I will, however, lay before you a much less complex economic principle:

Industry pays debts, while despair increases them.
—Poor Richard's, July 1757

So then, why this essay on Keynesian economics? Today, with your government exercising those monetary and fiscal actions—interest rates at record lows, hundreds of billions of dollars in stimulus expenditures—elucidated in Keynes's General Theory, America's economy remains in the doldrums, with high unemployment and meager growth in the domestic consumption of goods and services. Hence, some of those presently in high positions argue that Keynesian economics does not work, and America's economic problems would be best attacked by slashing most all government expenditures, thereby reducing the National Deficit.

I would suggest, for your consideration, that arguing Keynesian economics is flawed because America's economy has not responded to your government's monetary and fiscal initiatives is not dissimilar to wondering why a plaster cast applied to the leg of a patient does not cure his failing heart.

Keynesian economics promotes relief to cyclical business dips, not downward graveyard spirals. When drafting his General Theory, Keynes did not anticipate a nation in a steady deficit mode of existence. A jolt of additional borrowing and spending can help to fill America's most-recent economic dip, but it is impotent when laid against decades of merry spending, with a legacy of towering debt and interest payments that stretch over the horizon, toward China.

It be true then, I do believe, that Keynesian economics is not mending America's economic hurts, although, dear reader, it is rendering the hurts less so—"it" being the Stimulus Package that was painfully delivered via breech birth in 2009. If this be so, that the Stimulus Package does indeed lessen the economic hardships laid upon Americans, now is not the time to randomly cut Federal Expenditures. But, it *is* time to cut unnecessary expenditures. Oh, so easy to write! The words flow without effort or consequence. Let me cease grading eggs and attempt to lay a few . . . an image quite awkward and displeasing to envision. Nevertheless, for America's consideration:

- Do not cut unemployment benefits; do cease sending nine billion dollars in economic aid each year to an All Sand No Grass nation, when several billion of those dollars quickly ricochet into private accounts in Zurich, Dubai, and the South of France.
- Do not cut school lunch programs; do cease spending money to feed America's wild horses, the mustangs.
- Do not cut the FAA safety enforcement offices; do cease sending fifty (yes, fifty) planeloads of helicopters, cars, and equipment to support each of the President's international travels.

- Do not cut programs that repair and maintain America's highways and bridges; but do cease spending taxpayer money to fund the development of supersonic corporate jets, golf-course sprinkler systems, Shakespearean festivals, a study on why young men do not like condoms, and a study of grandparents' roles in Alaska (perhaps willing grandparents could assist in the latter study).

Yes, these last few are all programs funded by America's $700 billion Stimulus Package. One might ask, why would Congress include such bizarre projects in the Stimulus Package? The following excerpt from a *Poor Richard's Almanack* of 257 years ago could well explain, even more so if the last word of the quote, *money*, is replaced with *votes*.

He that is of the opinion money will do everything
may well be suspected of doing everything for money.
—Poor Richard's, July 1753

And, citizens, when you attempt to curtail Federal Expenditures, be forewarned: The Great Federal Beast will not be easily caged. It will strike back. It will be cunning. Recall 1995, when the White House and Congress failed to agree on a new budget, thus not feeding the Great Federal Beast. Rather than lying still, the Beast immediately closed our most prized National Parks, and the media excitedly broadcast videos of American families in their packed vans and campers being turned away from their much-anticipated holidays. The Great Federal Beast was then quickly fed. It will be no less cunning this time.

*   *   *

A few of my essays conclude with a counterpoint. I truly wish such an opposing viewpoint could end this essay, to temper my foreboding. But, alas, these concluding paragraphs only render worse that which appears already to be the worst.

While America must cease funding nonsensical and unproductive programs, such restraint will only serve to delay, not avoid, a financial paroxysm. There are fundamental structural problems with America's finances and national programs. And, dear Americans, know well that these structural problems—problems with a great span of digits preceded by a dollar sign—are not easily fixed with a sound bite uttered by a well-tanned and -clothed politician. Neither "Cut taxes" nor "Stop shipping jobs overseas" will serve as a cure-all elixir.

Two of the largest cracked and sagging beams in America's structure are Social Security and Medicare. Today your citizens live longer, but they do not work longer. Logic dictates, then, that their retirement years are longer; their need—their held-close-to-their-heart right—to draw monies from underfunded Social Security will be yet another tidal wave in a sea of debt. And, as laid before you in a previous essay, one reason Americans live longer into retirement is the application of greater and greater doses of health-care technology; this expanding end-of-life health care is most often paid for by Medicare. Know with a bleak certitude that future deficits from Social Security and Medicare may require the economic implosion of 2008 and 2009 to relinquish its current title as the worst financial calamity since the Great Depression.

With no less energy and commitment than when America declared war on Germany and Japan in 1941 and quickly reshaped America's economic landscape—children saved their pennies, and those not joining the military worked smarter, longer, and harder—the President and Congress must take action, the first being to acknowledge America's harsh fiscal realities and discard single-sentence soothing solutions.

CHILDREN

. . . God's Gift, or the Devil's Amusement

Of most topics set forth in this almanack I speak with a fair weight of confidence, a confidence born from life's experiences. And while I trust this confidence does not trespass to either boasting or intellectual bravado, there is one subject, one component of the human experience, that I am most ill-advised to speak of: the raising of children to the status of noble citizens. Even though my almanacks of 250 years ago were resplendent in sayings and truisms to guide a parent . . . *spare the rod, spoil the child* . . . I was not, if my only son to reach adulthood is a measure, a parent standing most proud. And while I take great comfort in my dear Sally, and the grandchildren she did provide, it is the loss that is most carefully measured and remembered within the human mind, not the gain.

In a previous essay I spoke to you of my son Franky, who died at four years of age, and his older sister Sarah . . . my Sally. Two years before Franky was born to my world, William was granted to me as my firstborn. While not as studious as I wished, and while his titled positions as a man sprang forth from the grace of my offices, William did no harm, caused no shame to be laid upon the Franklin name, until the War of Independence; then, his most vitriolic ruling from a throne of personal convenience and security. An excerpt from a letter to my son William, written by his round-shouldered, brokenhearted father:

> *Nothing has ever hurt me so much and affected me with such keen sensations, as to find myself deserted in my old age by my only son; and not only deserted, but to find him taking up arms against me in a cause wherein my good fame, fortune, and life are all at stake.*

What betrayal by William would cause a father to write such? As President of the Associated Loyalists he, my son, the son of a signatory of the Declaration of Independence, ordered the hanging of captured American militia; then, as a traitor to America wanted for murder, William fled to the safety of England.

As parents we endeavor to mold God's gifts into beings of virtue, truth, and honest labors. But as I wrote to my English friend Jonathan Shipley after America's independence had been won:

> When we launch our little fleet of barks into the ocean, bound to different ports, we hope for each a prosperous voyage. But contrary winds, hidden shoals, storms, and enemies come in for a share in the disposition of events; and though these occasion a mixture of disappointment, yet considering the risk where we can make no insurance, we should think ourselves happy if some return with success.

Parents should not despair; much is beyond our reach. Events and passions conspire to render our most prized behests from God as hostages to misbegotten, and even vile, principles; we must take solace in our lives for that which is right, that which is of merit . . . yes, they are God's gift.

CHINA SEEKS TO SELL PRODUCTS TO OTHER COUNTRIES

... Thus Bringing Opportunities to Its Workers

... WHILE ...

AMERICA SEEKS TO BRING STABILITY AND PROSPERITY TO OTHER COUNTRIES

... Thus Spending the Tax Dollars of Its Workers

I ask for the pardon of those typesetters, pressmen, composers, editors, and publishers among you. I have titled this essay not with a single title, but with two. Certainly, not a proper presentation of printed matter. But, the weight of this essay, not in word count, but in its most somber message, perhaps allows for two titles.

Now my thoughts—better stated, my most frightful worries—regarding China. Allow me, hopefully in a manner not too laborious, to first paint the background scenes before the players enter.

As I recounted in an earlier essay, to better comprehend the majesty of America's financial institutions, I meandered among those great Manhattan stone-and-glass castles of Goldman, Morgan, Merrill, and Citi, all protected by thick-walled fortifications manned by saber-toothed lawyers. During my days of observing Wall Street I came to know the comparisons and contrasts between Public Companies and Private Companies.

Alas, the Publicly Traded Company has numbers of mean-spirited constituents that it must hold at bay: the Internal Revenue Service, the Securities and Exchange Commission, Sarbanes-Oxley compliance officers, the Stock Exchange, an audit firm, the board of directors, various securities analysts, and, last but not least annoying, a few thousand shareholders, each one clinging tight to their "ownership rights."

A Private Company has far fewer constituents—perhaps only the IRS and a small number of docile private shareholders that comprise, most often, the board of directors, directors not burdened by complying with a few hundred pages of SEC, Stock Exchange, and Sarbanes-Oxley regulations. Neither is management threatened by lawsuits from minority shareholders, nor does it have to plead the merits of business decisions to securities analysts of little wisdom.

Obviously, dear reader, the Publicly Traded Company has far more audiences to placate than the private organization. Thus, the Public Corporation possesses far less flexibility in responding to business threats and opportunities. For your consideration, permit me to tender one example:

Shareholders of the Publicly Traded Company assume—demand—that over time the value of their stock holdings will, as a great oak, grow season after season. To fulfill this expectation the Company must increase its earnings; earnings are reported quarterly, ergo, management applies heroic efforts and, at times, accounting falsehoods, to, as you would say, "hit the numbers" each quarter. Quarterly objectives are short-term objectives. Even though managers might wish to retrench with certain product offerings and redeploy capital for an enhanced product, or strategy, they may be fearful that such action might cause them to miss quarterly earnings targets, thus requiring senior managers to relinquish their noble titles, chests of gold, swords, and corporate aircraft.

Within a Private Company the management is not burned at the stake for making long-term strategic decisions that negatively impact short-term earnings; its management team is consumed with a singular task: building a robust company.

Thus the *private company* has much more flexibility in positioning *itself* for long-term prosperous success than does a *publicly traded company.*

Pause for a moment, and consider the above sentence with three exchanged terms.

Thus a *dictatorship* has much more flexibility in positioning a *country* for long-term prosperous success than does a *democracy*.

Treasonous words, I know. But permit me to plead my supposition. Consider, my dear voter, that a democracy is governed by elected officials. Those American elected officials at the federal level, depending on which office they cling to, face the gauntlet of reelection every two, four, or six years. During relatively short tenures between election cycles, the wary officials often cast legislative votes that, in no small weight, are based on not alienating their constituents, versus what may be best for the long-term prospects of America.

And when the most senior American elected leader, the one with helicopters alighting in his backyard, attempts to legislate a progressive economic program, or other programs that the leader confidently believes are necessary for America's well-being, there is often a need to compromise—dilute and pollute—the strengths of proposed legislation to garner bipartisan support from congressional members, each and every one of whom has goals that are, even for a single congressional member, at odds with one another: Do what is best for my country, my state, my constituents, my party, my reelection?

A dictator only has one constituent to placate, that being the one in the mirror. And, as with the Private Company, the dictator may focus on long-term goals; no need to please voters with short-term results.

So, skeptical reader, you ask, why then have so many dictatorships, which possess key advantages over democracies, stagnated or failed? Perhaps two reasons. First, those aspiring to be a dictator—a Hitler or a Stalin—are often self-absorbed and possess a belief they are infallible—"If I were not, how could I have risen to the level of being my country's unquestioned leader?"—answerable to no one. From this position they exercise raw, unbridled power (invade thy neighbors), and in doing such, rarely seek counsel, lest they show weakness (not a desirable dictator attribute). Dictators, in time, become paranoid. The need to eradicate any real or perceived criticism becomes paramount; thus, more and more national resources are utilized to monitor and control the masses.

Another reason that totalitarian governments fail to blossom is that most dictators rose from the ranks of "workers," with the support of those very same workers. By nature, thus, they are hesitant to employ knowledgeable and educated administrators (elitists) to govern everyday affairs. Those administrators who are appointed demonstrate many of the attributes of their boss, the dictator; hence, they are risk-averse. Never wishing to make a mistake, they take no action—not a desirable quality for nation building.

Now I ask, if I may, that you sit up straight and absorb carefully and fully the words that follow—words that together form, I believe, one of the most critical messages of my essays. There is no doubt, there is no debate, that the People's Republic of China is unlike any nation the world has ever seen. It is neither a democracy nor a totalitarian country. China is a Private Company. A marvelously well-run Private Company. Its management team is the Chinese government. A Chinese government with no shareholder or voter constituents. Make no mistake, China is a brilliantly designed economic juggernaut designed to deliver an Armageddon . . . an Armageddon not for China, but an Armageddon designed to lay waste to other nations.

Frightful reader, China learned well from Russia; it learned the path not to take. Russia viewed America as its enemy . . . recall that in a previous essay I expounded upon Premier Khrushchev booming out to the world that Russia would bury America. For decades Russia matched America escalation by escalation in the arms race. Thousands of intercontinental-range missiles, tens of thousands of aircraft, thousands of tanks, hundreds of warships, hundreds of thousands of troops, billions and billions of dollars. While Russia could match America's military production and technology, it did not have the underlying national economy to afford its military might. Russia collapsed. Not a shot was fired. America's profitable, expanding businesses generating corporate taxes, together with more than a hundred million workers paying personal taxes, allowed America to outspend Russia . . . breaking it in the arms race.

At this time of its national evolution China does not covet the mantle of the world's dominant military power. Rather, China has adroitly positioned itself to become the world's colossal economic power. Forty years ago it began a journey to economic dominance with a potential workforce of 800 million. While undertrained, its workers were trainable. And given the bare standard of living for the average Chinese family, offering limited incremental income for long hours in factories was a seductive and powerful motivator, thus driving the nation's economic engine with hundreds of millions of smiling, exhausted workers.

China's massive workforce is directed by an enlightened totalitarian government, enlightened in that, unlike Soviet Russia's benighted government, which dreamt of "burying America," China's enlightened government has for its unstated dream the "buying of America." A goal to be accomplished over decades with incremental moves . . . training, educating, building, technology transfers, strategic raw material acquisitions, monetary manipulation, and exercising financial entrapment by being the eager lender to the world's Great Purchaser, America.

If I may, let me spread before you what I believe, after much studying of the matter, to be key components of China's strategy to crush America, and how it will implement this strategy:

- China dribbles out upward mobility to an immense workforce. If citizens work hard they can own a bike . . . a few years later, their own scooter . . . then a motorcycle . . . a car . . . an apartment. Decade after decade, by establishing higher goals against greater rewards, China rides the galloping horse of a motivated workforce.
- Many American workers already enjoy a standard of living several-fold better than a Chinese worker. They own homes, two cars, and flat-screen TVs . . . likely made in China. Upward mobility is more difficult (impossible) to promise the American worker in turn for heroic efforts of productivity.
- Because China began with a cheap—low-expectation—workforce, there is no need to have expansive social programs. Programs do exist, but only those that

contribute to productivity: free child care, work-place health care.

- American workers carry Himalaya-sized burdens of past and current federal programs . . . programs that do little, if anything, for productivity. They carry these burdens as tax dollars they pay on income they earn.
- The cold, harsh reality of all of the above is that China can produce items well below the cost of most American manufacturers. Thus, much as with Giles explaining to Warren several essays ago that lions pay leopards to hunt for them, Americans pay China to make things for them. At first the items were of no challenge; now they are the most technologically advanced. (A digression: The vast majority of Americans do not know that China has orbited men in space, a technological achievement not matched by England, France, Germany, or a hundred other countries.)
- China's government finances the expansion of developing Chinese companies so that they can better respond to global demands. This program, "economic security," allows such companies to expand their world market share.
- America's government only finances bankrupt companies that have proven their incompetency. These are referred to as "bailouts."
- China's government, using its national wealth and leverage, enters into relationships with other countries to gain long-term access to national resources—oil, coal, copper.

- Your free-enterprise America allows corporations to negotiate the purchase of raw material; such corporations negotiate contracts that maximize their short-term profits rather than securing America's best long-term interests.
- China's government orchestrates purchases for itself and Chinese companies that provide access to new technologies; it acquires aircraft from Boeing contingent upon Boeing building a plant in China to assemble the aircraft, thus transferring skills to Chinese companies and workers.
- American companies eat their young. Often for a few years of heightened profits they disclose, then transfer, their expertise and technologies to China.

The devil sweetens poison with honey.
　　　　　　　　　—Poor Richard's, *November 1747*

- Those technologies China cannot purchase, it steals. Yes, steals. Your FBI consumes more energy thwarting Chinese business espionage than it does with all other countries combined.
- China artificially manipulates the value of its currency to assure appropriate trade advantages. The yuan remains low, cheap, so that Chinese products benefit from a favorable exchange rate of currencies.
- Like a Vegas cocktail waitress plying a blackjack player with free drinks (yes, dear reader, I have visited Vegas), China lends America money: China

buys bonds issued by our Treasury; a portion of the borrowed money is recycled through federal programs (bridge building, unemployment payments), and the dollars ultimately flow to individual Americans who, with a few of the dollars, go to the mall and purchase goods made in China.

- China is the largest holder of Treasury bonds. If the total owed China is divided by the number of Americans, including those in cradles, each American needs to write a check to the People's Republic of China (credit cards most likely not accepted) for $2,800. For children without checking accounts, parents will need to add their children's repayments to their reimbursement checks.

- China expends substantial monies to educate its brightest—and many are bright—at the best schools in the world. Because China is paying for their education, it dictates their areas of study; China places heavy emphasis on the sciences and engineering.

- America has a financially fragile student loan program, and recipients are free to select their area of study; thus, your American educational subsidies help to finance the education of armies of lawyers and other professions that seek to make money on transactions, versus producing those goods that create transactions.

- China is not burdened with a significant national debt; it does not step forward as America does to fund one world cause after another. However, China does allocate a small portion of its bureaucracy to draft critiques and complaints of America's initiatives to assist other countries.

- While China's military is large enough to cause any nation to pause, it is only a small portion of that of America. China feels no need to protect other nations from threats. It annually spends $100 billion on defense, America, $600 billion.

- When China has the opportunity on the world stage to lend its weight to containing a bubbling international crisis, often it remains comfortably quiet. Better the crisis keeps bubbling and our America keeps spending its resources on making the world safe . . . safe for China to sell its products.

- China manufactures products for American companies that are marketed to the world as American products. Thus, the American companies—Nike, Hewlett-Packard, only two of hundreds—generate corporate profits for themselves. There will come a time, as the leopards looked at the lions and asked why they were hunting for them, that China will market the products directly, meaning no corporate profits for the American company.

- To the above dire prediction, American businesses quickly argue that China has no American marketing expertise, nor does it possess brand names. Sounds reassuring—as reassuring as when Philco smugly claimed that no one would buy a Japanese television, or when General Motors executives boasted that every American man's dream was to own a Cadillac.

In another decade, concerned reader, China will possess each and every piece of technology known in the world. The Chinese will have a military, while not as large as America's, large enough to lay waste to any nation; thus, they will fear no one. Behind the thick walls of their central bank will be piles of IOUs from America, in the trillions. While Americans may take comfort by reassuring themselves that China, in time, will undergo a revolution, its citizens clamoring for democracy, and when achieved, China will become docile and nonthreatening . . . perhaps not. The Chinese government has demonstrated, as a fisherman might play out a line to a hooked and thrashing fish, how to trickle out upward economic mobility to its citizens, creating an energetic population; hence, one might reasonably expect that this same government would be no less clever with human rights, trickling them out over decades to create not only an energetic population, but a tranquil population. Thus, in a score of years China will possess a stable hardworking population as large as America, Japan, Great Britain, and Germany combined. A hardworking population that benefits from all the technologies of the world.

The United States has to move fast to even stand still.

—John F. Kennedy

While America's leaders warn of the war on terror, there is another enemy. An enemy that will bring Americans to their knees as we brought Russians to theirs; not by military might, but by assembling the most robust economy the world has ever seen, this done while American leaders seek to stabilize the world by offering other countries, both great and small, financial carrots to remain tranquil, carrots bought by American taxpayers, or bought with debt payable by future American taxpayers.

America is peering in the wrong direction to see its greatest challenges; it is playing the wrong game. Yet, kind sirs and ladies, it is no game.

AMERICA, YOU CAN DO IT

. . . You the Congress, President, and Citizens

Many challenges, many threats have confronted the citizens of America since its inception. And at the very moment of our Country's birth, with signatures of wet ink on the Declaration of Independence, America faced its greatest challenge. Our thirteen Colonies held just over two million souls. From these Colonies stood, in ragged lines, an untrained militia of only a few thousand. With these few we declared a fight with—we dared to fight—no less than the strongest of nations, England. An England of might, with a fearful army of Redcoats and a navy of two hundred ships . . . America had five. And England possessed another wondrous advantage, a Treasury of gold and wealth; enough to finance a war, enough to pay other nations to join the fight against the American quilt of Colonies. A quilt held together by a few thin threads of hope; hope of what could be. So, dear reader, while today's challenges are great, greater challenges have been beaten into submission by strong-willed, brave-hearted Americans.

I know that many of the essays laid before you in this narrative were broken-glass sharp. Too sharp, if the truth of the matter be known. But the written word does not allow a voice to be raised; the written exhortation does not convey the tremble in the voice of a worried messenger, nor a sentry warning of doom. Sharp words were my trembling voice, so do not take offense.

I ask that you consider my opening words to this transmittal: "Let me acknowledge what a truly admirable nation of citizens populate America." Today, no less than ever, citizens of other countries admire and, yes, covet much of what is America. And one such admirable quality of America is that ability to look inward and exercise constant hand-wringing over America's faults, many of these faults being only the less-than-perfect execution of attempting to do right for all; not an all for America, but an all for the world.

Let me set aside my plaudits for today's American citizens; let me instead be a quorum of one presenting in boldface America's greatest problem: **Congress**. America has an array of challenges: energy, debt, ecology, defense, immigration, education, plus scores of others discussed thus far. The solutions to these problems, or the foundations to the solutions, reside in passing constructive legislation in Congress, such legislation to be sculpted by a single eye—an eye for America's best interests.

To fault those elected officials in Congress for the nation's dysfunctional governance is not a fair indictment. While there have been individual abuses of power, and while too often partisanship trumps patriotism, Congress possesses a congenital flaw that renders America's legislative body with a rigor mortis. Those elected officials of Congress suffer from entrapment. Realities under which they serve often coerce them to take paths of necessity, not patriotic service.

In my America, if one owned a horse, or could borrow a neighbor's horse, one could run for Congress. The hopeful candidates rode from village to village, and from village to town. At each village or town center they sought a small rise, a stump, or other perch to stand tall and convey, in a strong voice, a message crafted by their well-paid pollsters, media coaches, and issue specialists (sorry, I could not contain my satiric voice). Those gathered around a candidate could measure his words (yes, they were his words, never her words) and call out questions. As the citizens learned about the candidate, the candidate learned firsthand about the citizens' needs and fears.

Today a newly elected congressman or congresswoman arrives in Washington brimming with patriotism and a sense of duty. With much ceremony, the new representatives are sworn in to office with their proud spouses by their sides, and then the waves roll in; waves of realities that wash away the patriotic sand castles in their minds. Representatives are advised by the Party's whip—the drill sergeant to the platoon of new recruits—that future congressional committee assignments will be based on Party loyalty and adherence to the dictates of the congressional leadership. If they are strong Party loyalists, the Party will transport bundles of monies to their districts for their reelection. They are told they need to raise $1 to $5 million for their next campaign, and the primary campaigns will begin in sixteen months. Soon smiling lobbyists invite the fresh-faced representative to a duck shoot on the Eastern Shore of Maryland, to a luxury box at a Redskins game, or, perhaps, to a round of golf at the Congressional Country Club . . . just to get to know them better, no other agenda. In time friends of the lobbyists appear at these outings—corporate friends of the lobbyists. Corporate friends either for or against some pending legislation. Corporate friends who, with their lobbyists providing hors d'oeuvres and drinks, host fund-raisers for the representative. Corporate friends who direct the flow of Political Action Committee contributions, barrels of monies corporations raise from their employees, for the representative's upcoming election.

A horse and a tree stump no longer carry the day. To obtain office, to retain office, today's candidate must raise monies; for the 435 representatives in Congress, $1 to $5 million for general elections every two years. Thus, a successful representative in Congress must be an energetic fund-raiser, and know well that the ability to raise funds is hindered or helped by whether the representative conforms to the expectations of the Party and donors.

In my introduction I acknowledged how it was "immodest of me to pen essays that expound upon your faults and problems." Permit me to be even more immodest as I suggest, in a manner I trust not too pretentious or too imbued with unfettered arrogance, my plan to remedy this unhealthy preponderance of special interests steering and manipulating our legislative branch of government. For your consideration I recommend the following course in order to counter and lay limp this greatest threat to America, these nearly omnipotent corporations exercising their mountain-range-sized fiscal bulk as if they were the fourth branch of government. Permit me to suggest how to render our Congress once again a constructive force in crafting legislation to confront, confound, and solve America's problems. We begin with the lobbyists.

Weighty questions ask for deliberate answers.
—Poor Richard's, *April 1735*

So then, how do we put corporate lobbyists out of business (a few are presently in jail) and tell Corporate America to keep its money, thus returning to the three branches of government the Founding Fathers envisioned? Please, sit up. America needs a Twenty-eighth Constitutional Amendment. An amendment to provide horses and tree stumps. And unlike most challenges facing America, repairing Congress will require little effort, other than the will to make the change.

Do not squirm or flinch. I am not suggesting America undertake anything not done before. There have been many amendments to our Constitution; many have dealt with voting, elections, and terms of office. So what I suggest—a play on a word to follow—is not revolutionary; rather, it is evolutionary. An evolutionary change necessary for the legislative body to productively survive the changing environment of America.

If we attempted to place more-stringent campaign spending limits on candidates, ways around these prohibitions would quickly be found. Rather, let us place the money on the table for all to see. Let the money come from the taxpayer. We established earlier in these essays that American taxpayers pay for everything in the end anyway. Bear in mind that when MasterCard, McDonald's, and Pfizer pay their lobbyists tens of millions of dollars, the executives of these firms don't reach into their waistcoat pockets for the money; instead, the cost of your MasterCard, your Big Mac, and those little blue pills, and in fact, the cost of most every product sold by American corporations, goes to pay Washington lobbyists. You, the American consumers, are paying the lobbyists, albeit indirectly; you provide the monies from the products you purchase. Corporate America writes the check to the lobbyist and thereby acquires and exercises influence with your monies.

What would be the cost to Americans to fund the campaigns of Congress directly? About $10 per household each year would be the meager expense. Do you not think it's a staggeringly low sum to pay for unbiased representation dedicated to protecting and promoting the voters' interests rather than the interests of mighty corporations?

In concert with tendering all representatives campaign monies, consider a change in their term. It takes many new representatives months to find the restrooms of the Capitol. Should not we give them more than a two-year term to become productive patriots? Perhaps a constitutional amendment providing three years would be both practical and more consistent with the senator's term of six years. And speaking of senators, they should benefit from the same campaign financing as the representatives.

Would each American family be willing to pay twenty cents a week to have a Congress beholden to them, and not to the banking industry, the defense industry, the oil and gas industry, the medical and drug industry, the telecommunications industry, the insurance industry—the list goes on. Recall the 2003 Medicare drug legislation: If our government had carved out a mere single-percentage-point discount on the $50 billion it spends on drugs for the elderly, the savings would have offset the twenty cents a week by many multiples.

As long as our thoughts are within that great domed Capitol, another problem should be addressed; it is the behavior of certain Congressional Members. Behavior that at times is immoral, unprofessional, unpatriotic, and fraudulent. With today's media coverage of the trivial, trite, and trashy, you likely know of the senator sleeping with his aide's wife, the congressman who keeps cash bribes in his freezer, and the chairman of the committee overseeing tax legislation who forgot to pay all his taxes . . . we have already pulled the scab off Medicare. But let's consider another problem perhaps no less troublesome: Most often when offenses by members of Congress involving untoward behavior are made known, a Congressional Ethics Committee, composed of peers of the offenders, sits in judgment and almost always administers only a whispered admonishment or a gentle tap on the wrist.

> *You may give a man an Office, but you cannot give him Discretion.*
>
> —Poor Richard's, *August 1754*

Every one of our young Americans attending a military academy must adhere, with no tolerance allowed, no' exceptions permitted, to a strict Honor Code. These young cadets and middies are quickly dismissed for any misstep. Their Code requires that no one shall lie, cheat, steal, or tolerate those who do. A summary as follows:

LYING: *Shall not deceive another by stating an untruth or by telling of a partial truth or ambiguous use of information or language with the intent to deceive.*

CHEATING: *Shall not act out of self-interest or assist another to do so with the intent to gain or give an unfair advantage.*

STEALING: *Shall not deprive or defraud another person, or others, of the use and benefit of property, or to appropriate it to the use of any person other than the owner.*

Should not our Congress agree to the same standard of moral conduct as those young persons in our military academies? Is this too much to ask?

So, then, to repair Congress and allow those representatives and senators to "do the people's work," a constitutional amendment is suggested that would provide 100 percent of the campaign funds necessary for both the incumbent and challenger to finance their campaigns. Also, for your consideration, I suggest a modification to the oaths of office in such a manner that each member of Congress agrees to abide by those same ethical and moral standards as our young men and women in America's military academies.

One Mendfault is worth two Findfaults, but one Findfault is better than two Makefaults.
—Poor Richard's, December 1735

Now, for the presidency. But first a paragraph of heartfelt emotion and awe. The life story of today's President is America's story. For both, from meager circumstances great obstacles were overcome. Obstacles overcome against odds that most rational individuals would have claimed made success impossible. Odds that seemed to render failure predestined. But persistence, persistence in doing that which was right, overcame all. Overcame all by heroic efforts and staying the course. Thirteen Colonies populated by the descendants of immigrants became the greatest Country of the world. An African American youngster with a strange name and an absentee father in time became the President of the United States. Know well that the preceding sentence was made possible only by that sentence that preceded it.

Permit me to dry my eyes. To the point of this essay. Mr. President, you possess a keen intellect, you have benevolent and sympathetic intentions, and most citizens are proud to have you represent America on the world stage. But, if I may, permit me to restate a portion of my letter of introduction:

> *Those kindhearted benevolent qualities of America, those sterling attributes that are such a part of your greatness, will if not bridled with financial restraint and reasonableness cause "Greatest" to slowly fade from our Country's honored title.*

As America cannot afford to address all the world's problems, neither can it address those problems of its citizens that are best addressed by individual citizens. As with all things, words to instruct drip easily; actions to implement, a thick molasses. This molasses turns increasingly viscous the more uncertainty there is between that which is the Country's collective responsibility and that which is the citizen's individual responsibility.

At the risk of being too immodest, let me recount a story from my tenure on your good Earth. At seventeen years of age, the year was 1723, I broke away from my half brother's printing business and journeyed to Philadelphia, thus leaving my family behind in Boston. In time I saw an opportunity to establish my own printing business in Philadelphia. I returned home, and with a letter of support and promise from the Governor of Pennsylvania, I approached my father; I asked him for a small loan to start my own printing business. He thought on the matter for several days. He then told me no. What I knew would be an enterprise of good commerce he denied me; my father denied me my opportunity.

I returned to Philadelphia discouraged. Then, armed with entrepreneurial promises of money, I journeyed to England. There these promises were broken, marooning me so that I had to work again for meager pay in print shops owned by others. After two years of hard labor and frugality I managed to return to America. With Hugh Meredith as a partner, together we began a small printing business. I worked long hours, he drank long hours. After one year I bought out his share of our business. Six years after my father denied me my dream, I was nevertheless living my dream. If my father had granted me the loan, would my life's happiness have been greater? No. Would my life's happiness have been less so? I think certainly yes.

And permit me to quickly testify that my life was productive not only for what my father didn't provide, but for what he did provide. He provided what he should have: a home of taught values, a home of frugality. If these gifts had not been tendered to me in my youth, whether he had acquiesced to the loan requested or not, my life would never have been the one I embraced, lived to the fullest, and so cherished.

Mr. President, you are the Captain of a great ship that, I humbly warn, is sinking. It was sinking when you became Captain. Large gaping holes below the waterline had been smashed open by rocky shoals of naive benevolence, staggering incompetence, and, yes, greed. Mr. President—cease regaling the passengers with pleasing tales and uplifting visions of happy visits at future ports of call at palm-tree-studded islands; grab a megaphone, tell all to follow your lead, and take immediate action to stem the flow.

And be forearmed, Mr. President: Those within the great Federal Beast will not easily capitulate to tempering federal expenditures. Neither will many of your American citizens. Actions to reduce spending will be met by voices screaming of the hurt, the misery you are causing. But as my father, a father who loved me, denied me the money I sought, so must you for America. Brace yourself.

> *He that would rule must hear, but be deaf; he must see, but be blind.*
>
> —Author unknown

Take comfort, Mr. President, in knowing that if you go to the people, if you speak frankly about what must be done, most will understand. But, please do not speak of consensus building. Do not speak of all those that have good ideas; do not speak of America's greatness, or of America's wonderfully diverse population. No; instead, speak of what must be done. Speak of firmly curtailing expenditures knowing that Americans crave a strong leader. And no matter how harsh the message, if delivered with a singular purpose, and with confidence and conviction, it will be embraced by most citizens.

> *The secret to rulership is to combine a belief in one's infallibility with the power to learn from past mistakes.*
>
> —George Orwell, 1984

My fellow citizens, it is your life. It is your responsibility to make your life a productive one. Yes, I know that many of you did the right things. You worked, you saved, you voted, you prayed. Now you suffer. For this I am truly sorry. But your government cannot make it right. Your government, the source of much of the problem, is itself fragile, too fragile because it tried to "make it right" for too many—too many who needed to create their own happiness, not look to their government to provide it gratis.

While you cannot ask your government for help, you can first stymie, then eradicate Corporate America's influence on our Congress . . . yes, it is *our* Congress . . . the people's Congress, not Corporate America's Congress. Support, demand, that the Twenty-eighth Constitutional Amendment be passed into law. Or, contrive another measure to defend Congress from an army of lobbyists.

But, take action; do not merely hope that others will.

He that lives on Hope, dies farting.
                                   —Poor Richard's, *February 1736*

FINAL THOUGHTS

... TILL NEXT YEAR

While I have been caustic in many of my essays, an even greater offense has been my intemperate prejudicial remarks . . . laying negative attributes of a few across the entirety of a group of individuals and institutions. Permit me to mend my ways.

Corporations are not evil. Most struggle to tender competitive products and services, and most corporate officers and members of their boards of directors are truly fine human beings. So it be with religious leaders, whose lives are most often dedicated to doing God's work. So it be with your Congress; most all of those who serve in the greatest legislative body of the greatest nation seek to do only things that are best for Americans. So it be with your President, who, with his intelligence and magnanimous benevolence, endeavors to do the greatest good for America. And certainly it be for you citizens of America, who struggle to build a life of contentment for your family while offering a hand to those in need, near and far.

And please know well that my essays laid before you, and the conclusions they constructed, were chosen to convey my thoughts only. No leaning, no bias, did I intend; neither conservative nor liberal, Republican or Democrat, Honker or Quacker, Real or Unreal. If you choose to classify my writing with a single descriptor, please be advised that as beauty is in the eye of the beholder, and prejudice in the mind of the beholder, your classification of my thoughts exists solely in your mind . . . not in mine.

My heartfelt appreciation is herewith tendered. I thank you for pondering my messages and for considering my call to action. You are truly the most noble citizens, the most kindhearted citizens, of our good Earth.

> *Who is wise? He who learns from everyone.*
> *Who is powerful? He who governs his passions.*
> *Who is rich? He who is content.*
> *Who is that? Nobody.*
>
> —Poor Richard's, July 1755